T. LUCRETI CARI

DE RERUM NATURA

A SELECTION FROM THE FIFTH BOOK
(783–1457)

EDITED

WITH INTRODUCTION, ANALYSES AND NOTES

BY

W. D. LOWE, M.A.

FORMERLY SCHOLAR OF PEMBROKE COLLEGE, CAMBRIDGE
JUNIOR CENSOR, UNIVERSITY COLLEGE, DURHAM
EDITOR OF 'THE CENA TRIMALCHIONIS OF PETRONIUS ARBITER'
'TALES OF THE CIVIL WAR FROM CAESAR BELLUM CIVILE III'

OXFORD
AT THE CLARENDON PRESS
1907

HENRY FROWDE, M.A.
PUBLISHER TO THE UNIVERSITY OF OXFORD
LONDON, EDINBURGH
NEW YORK AND TORONTO

PREFACE

THIS edition has been prepared in the hope that with its help some of the finest and most vivid Latin poetry that survives may in the future be read in lower forms than has been hitherto usual.

There is a natural objection to reading part of a poem or to beginning in the middle of a book, and it is hoped that an edition which omits the preceding eight hundred lines, a long and difficult passage with no particular connexion with this selection, and which so presents a subject of more reasonable length for a middle form, will virtually if not actually remove such hesitation.

Though a selection, it is *totus teres atque rotundus* and forms a complete epic in itself. Lucretius is generally considered to be a difficult author and is reserved for the higher forms, but it is believed that this selection will, with the aid of the notes, be found to present little difficulty to the average boy, and it will certainly give him an intensely graphic picture of the development of civilization as conceived by the most imaginative genius among Latin writers. Every edition of Lucretius is based on Munro's great work, and this one owes much to Mr. Duff's admirable edition. I also offer my sincere thanks to the reader of the Clarendon Press for many instances of suggestive advice. The text of the Clarendon Press has been followed practically throughout.

W. D. LOWE.

THE CASTLE,
DURHAM, 1906.

A 2

CONTENTS

INTRODUCTION

THE LIFE OF LUCRETIUS

THE life of Lucretius, as it is usually accepted, is given here without any examination of the conflicting accounts and theories put forward by different editors.

Titus Lucretius Carus was born probably B.C. 99 and died October 15, B.C. 55. The statement that his death was due to suicide during madness brought on by drugs must be viewed with suspicion. He was a man of good family. He had literary tastes and showed no inclination for a political life, more especially during the troublous times of the struggles between Pompey and Caesar. He lived the life of a student and devoted himself to the philosophy of Epicurus : the result of his lifework is the presentation of that philosophy in the didactic poem *De Rerum Natura* in six books, a work that is not the production of a madman, whatever defects it may contain. Moreover, as Mr. Mackail in his *Latin Literature* says : ' Many of the most important physical discoveries of modern times are hinted at or even expressly stated by Lucretius.' Indeed his theories of the atomic doctrine, of light, of evolution and of the ultimate constitution of atoms have won the admiration of modern scientists.

THE STYLE OF LUCRETIUS

Lucretius was, at any rate in literature, *laudator temporis acti*. He admired and imitated the older poets : Homer and Empedocles among the Greeks, Ennius and the older tragedians among the Latin poets, were studied diligently by him and influenced his language and turn of expression strongly. He is fond of using old and half-forgotten forms of words : he uses and invents compound adjectives of a Greek type, such as *vulgivagus, levisomnus, anguimanus, pennipotens, bucerus :* alliteration and assonance, a characteristic feature in the early period of the literature of any nation, play a prominent part, especially where the poet wishes to drive a point home.

The Lucretian hexameter is distinctly in advance of that of Ennius, yet it is closer to the rugged verse of the older poet than to the smoothness and elaboration of the Vergilian line. He is ready to use spondaic endings, archaic terminations of substantives and verbs: he makes free use of elision and frequently marks off the

5

first two feet from the rest of the line, interrupting the rhythm by a sudden jerk. One of the especial features in the verse of Lucretius is his method of dealing with the fourth foot, which is frequently contained in a single word and ends with it, while Vergil prefers to have a caesura. For instance Vergil writes ' arma virumque cano Troiae qui primus ab oris,' inverting the natural order of *Troiae qui* : Lucretius would be content to retain the natural order *qui Troiae* and to dispense with the caesura which Vergil prefers to have. So in our passage Lucretius writes ' per totum corpus adhaesu, quod tantis viribus auctos, nix venti fulmina grando ' ; in these lines Vergil would probably have written ' totum per corpus adhaesu, tantis quod, venti nix.'

The poem leaves on the reader, and still more on the hearer, an impression of great vigour and freedom of expression untrammelled by the elaboration considered necessary by the later poets. Mr. Duff in his introduction aptly quotes the words of Munro : ' It has often struck me that his genius is akin to that of Milton. He displays a wonderful depth and fervour of thought, expressed in language of singular force and beauty ; an admirable faculty of clear, vigorous and well-sustained philosophical reasoning ; and a style equal in its purity and correctness to that of Terence, Caesar or Cicero, and superior to that of any writer of the Augustan age.'

Another great asset possessed by Lucretius is the imaginative insight and exuberant originality by which he pictures to himself and unfolds to his readers the long periods of the early struggles of mankind in the dim recesses of the past, until gradually they reached by the processes of evolution that development of civilization which culminated in the perfection of his own time (' ad summum donec venere cacumen ').

Mommsen closes his sketch of Lucretius with this tribute : ' The didactic poem concerning the Nature of Things, however much in it may challenge censure, has remained one of the most brilliant stars in the poorly illuminated expanse of Roman literature.'

THE PHILOSOPHY OF EPICURUS

Epicurus based his philosophy on the axiom that experience alone was the foundation-stone of certainty : experience is to be gained from the impressions of the senses : therefore sensation is the standard of truth. Moreover, he held that the study of Nature was desirable in so far as it freed mankind from the trammels of religion and superstition.

In Physics he denied divine agency in the creation of the world, maintaining that it was due to the collision and combinations of immutable and irreducible atoms, and that the meeting of these atoms was rendered possible by the existence of void. Similarly the soul itself is composed of the lightest atoms, and is therefore of the same nature as the body, though more agile through the excessive lightness of its composition ; yet it will perish with the body and will have no future existence as it, no less than the more material and tangible world, has no divine element.

In Ethics Epicurus held the view that pleasure is the sole good and pain the sole evil: pleasure is the absence of pain. Mental pleasures are the greater, for bodily pleasures are merely ephemeral. To ensure freedom from pain he taught the value of plain living, seeing in virtue not the end of life, but rather the means to the end of life, which offered to him a state of temperate equilibrium and pleasant tranquillity, both mental and physical (ἀταραξία). So in Ethics, no less than in Physics, we see that all idea of higher and more spiritual life is absent, that the divine element is again lacking.

What was a philosophy to the master became a religion to the disciple, and Lucretius in his enthusiastic admiration for Epicurus preached the gospel of Epicureanism more fervently than its founder, exclaiming from the depths of his heart 'deus ille fuit, deus' (bk. 5. 8).

THE POEM 'DE RERUM NATURA'

Lucretius wished to expound the doctrine of Epicurus not merely from a desire to put before his readers his physical system, but chiefly from a deeply rooted wish to free mankind from fear of the gods and from the terrors of death which are caused by the belief in a future life : he therefore determined to explain the true nature of things.

Books one and two describe fully the physical theories of Democritus and Epicurus, dwelling on the nature of atoms and void, the chief component parts of the universe. Book three shows that the soul is a material part of man and perishes when the body dies: the next deals with the Epicurean theory of sense. The fifth book describes the creation of the world, the evolution of man and the beginnings of society. In the last book Lucretius puts before us a number of natural phenomena and curiosities in nature, probably intending to rearrange and systematize them before it was actually published.

THE SUBJECT-MATTER OF THE FIFTH BOOK

The fifth book of Lucretius opens with a panegyric on Epicurus. The poet then promises a sketch of the creation of the world and of the heavenly bodies, in order that men realizing the mortal nature of the world may not be enslaved to the belief that it was created by the gods, who were in reality indifferent to the affairs of mankind and had no inducement to exchange their leisured happiness for the anxiety of world-making. Surely too, if the gods had made the world, it would have been both better and happier. To Lucretius Nature was the real creative power. The world and all that is in it is mortal; water, air, fire, stones, ether itself, all gradually decay and die away. Earth had its beginning and must have its end. He then goes on to describe the formation of the world out of indestructible atoms which collided and combined: the heavier particles forming the earth, the lighter ones composing the ether and the heavenly bodies, and so the earth sank and the ether rose. Next, he endeavours to describe the motions and courses of the stars and to explain the nature of the sun, which he with the Epicureans maintained was really of the size that it appeared to them. After this follows a description of the recurrence of days and nights, of the succession of the seasons, and an explanation of the causes of eclipses.

At this point our selection opens with the story of the creation of herbage, animals, birds, and lastly man produced from earth, the all-mother. Lucretius denies the possibility of beings of twofold nature, such as Centaurs, Satyrs, Scylla and the like. Then follows an account of the earliest life of man, the beginnings of social intercourse, the discovery of fire and the development of civilization. And now Lucretius launches out into a bitter indictment of religion and describes its evil effects on man. Next he tells of the discovery of the use of metals, the consequent development of war and its instruments, the cultivation of the soil, the beginnings of music, and the observance of the recurring seasons. Naturally resulting from these arts come the closer life and communion of man with man, the discovery of letters, the beginnings of history, and the progress of the arts and luxuries of life up to the elaborate civilization of his own day.

DE RERVM NATVRA
LIBER V

*Earth, the mother of all, produced first herbage, then animate
beings, birds, &c., lastly mankind. She also gave them natural
food, as a mother does to her child. In the early days the
seasons were temperate.*

PRINCIPIO genus herbarum viridemque nitorem
terra dedit circum collis camposque per omnis,
florida fulserunt viridanti prata colore,   785
arboribusque datumst variis exinde per auras
crescendi magnum immissis certamen habenis.
ut pluma atque pili primum saetaeque creantur
quadrupedum membris et corpore pennipotentum,
sic nova tum tellus herbas virgultaque primum   790
sustulit, inde loci mortalia saecla creavit
multa modis multis varia ratione coorta.
nam neque de caelo cecidisse animalia possunt
nec terrestria de salsis exisse lacunis.
linquitur ut merito maternum nomen adepta   795
terra sit, e terra quoniam sunt cuncta creata.
multaque nunc etiam exsistunt animalia terris
imbribus et calido solis concreta vapore ;
quo minus est mirum si tum sunt plura coorta
et maiora, nova tellure atque aethere adulta.   800
principio genus alituum variaeque volucres
ova relinquebant exclusae tempore verno,
folliculos ut nunc teretes aestate cicadae
linquunt sponte sua victum vitamque petentes.
tum tibi terra dedit primum mortalia saecla.   805
multus enim calor atque umor superabat in arvis.
hoc ubi quaeque loci regio opportuna dabatur,
crescebant uteri terram radicibus apti ;

9

quos ubi tempore maturo patefecerat aetas
infantum fugiens umorem aurasque petessens,   810
convertebat ibi natura foramina terrae
et sucum venis cogebat fundere apertis
consimilem lactis, sicut nunc femina quaeque
cum peperit, dulci repletur lacte, quod omnis
impetus in mammas convertitur ille alimenti.   815
terra cibum pueris, vestem vapor, herba cubile
praebebat multa et molli lanugine abundans.
at novitas mundi nec frigora dura ciebat
nec nimios aestus nec magnis viribus auras.
omnia enim pariter crescunt et robora sumunt.   820

*Mother earth has now in her old age ceased bearing. All
things gradually change and decay, even so it is with earth.*

Quare etiam atque etiam maternum nomen adepta
terra tenet merito, quoniam genus ipsa creavit
humanum atque animal prope certo tempore fudit
omne quod in magnis bacchatur montibu' passim,
aeriasque simul volucris variantibu' formis.   825
sed quia finem aliquam pariendi debet habere,
destitit, ut mulier spatio defessa vetusto.
mutat enim mundi naturam totius aetas
ex alioque alius status excipere omnia debet,
nec manet ulla sui similis res : omnia migrant,   830
omnia commutat natura et vertere cogit.
namque aliud putrescit et aevo debile languet,
porro aliud succrescit et e contemptibus exit.
sic igitur mundi naturam totius aetas
mutat et ex alio terram status excipit alter,   835
quod tulit ut nequeat, possit quod non tulit ante.

*The earth at first produced many monsters and monstrosities,
but fortunately nature did not allow these to propagate their
kind, and so they gradually died out again.*

Multaque tum tellus etiam portenta creare
conatast mira facie membrisque coorta,

10

androgynum, interutrasque nec utrum, utrimque remotum,
orba pedum partim, manuum viduata vicissim,   840
muta sine ore etiam, sine vultu caeca reperta,
vinctaque membrorum per totum corpus adhaesu,
nec facere ut possent quicquam nec cedere quoquam
nec vitare malum nec sumere quod foret usus.
cetera de genere hoc monstra ac portenta creabat,   845
nequiquam, quoniam natura absterruit auctum
nec potuere cupitum aetatis tangere florem
nec reperire cibum nec iungi per Veneris res.
multa videmus enim rebus concurrere debere,
ut propagando possint procudere saecla.   850

*Animals which did not possess some pre-eminent quality or
natural advantage soon became extinct and fell a prey to those
that were stronger and better fitted for the struggle for
existence. Others owe their preservation to their domestica-
tion by man.*

Multaque tum interiisse animantum saecla necessest 855
nec potuisse propagando procudere prolem.
nam quaecumque vides vesci vitalibus auris,
aut dolus aut virtus aut denique mobilitas est
ex ineunte aevo genus id tutata reservans.
multaque sunt, nobis ex utilitate sua quae   860
commendata manent, tutelae tradita nostrae.
principio genus acre leonum saevaque saecla
tutatast virtus, vulpis dolus et fuga cervos.
at levisomna canum fido cum pectore corda
et genus omne quod est veterino semine partum   865
lanigeraeque simul pecudes et bucera saecla
omnia sunt hominum tutelae tradita, Memmi.
nam cupide fugere feras pacemque secuta
sunt et larga suo sine pabula parta labore,
quae damus utilitatis eorum praemia causa.   870
at quis nil horum tribuit natura, nec ipsa
sponte sua possent ut vivere nec dare nobis

utilitatem aliquam quare pateremur eorum
praesidio nostro pasci genus esseque tutum,
scilicet haec aliis praedae lucroque iacebant   875
indupedita suis fatalibus omnia vinclis,
donec ad interitum genus id natura redegit.

Such strange monsters as Centaurs, Satyrs, Scylla, Chimaera,
&c., could never have existed outside the imagination: for in
these beings of twofold nature the maturity of the one part is
fully developed before the maturity of the other part; a horse
would be strong and vigorous while the human element would
still be tender, and again the horse would be old and beyond
work when the human element had just reached its strength.
So too trees and plants still retain their characteristics and
cannot at any rate beyond a certain limit be transformed.

Sed neque Centauri fuerunt, nec tempore in ullo
esse queunt duplici natura et corpore bino
ex alienigenis membris compacta, potestas   880
hinc illinc partis ut non par esse potissit.
id licet hinc quamvis hebeti cognoscere corde.
principio circum tribus actis impiger annis
floret equus, puer haudquaquam ; nam saepe etiam nunc
ubera mammarum in somnis lactantia quaeret.   885
post ubi equum validae vires aetate senecta
membraque deficiunt fugienti languida vita,
tum demum pueris aevo florente iuventas
occipit et molli vestit lanugine malas.
ne forte ex homine et veterino semine equorum   890
confieri credas Centauros posse neque esse,
aut rabidis canibus succinctas semimarinis
corporibus Scyllas et cetera de genere horum,
inter se quorum discordia membra videmus ;
quae neque florescunt pariter nec robora sumunt   895
corporibus neque proiciunt aetate senecta
nec simili Venere ardescunt nec moribus unis
conveniunt, neque sunt eadem iucunda per artus.
quippe videre licet pinguescere saepe cicuta

barbigeras pecudes, homini quae est acre venenum.   900
⟨denique⟩ flamma quidem cum corpora fulva leonum
tam soleat torrere atque urere quam genus omne
visceris in terris quodcumque et sanguinis exstet,
qui fieri potuit, triplici cum corpore ut una,
prima leo, postrema draco, media ipsa, Chimaera   905
ore foras acrem flaret de corpore flammam?
quare etiam tellure nova caeloque recenti
talia qui fingit potuisse animalia gigni,
nixus in hoc uno novitatis nomine inani,
multa licet simili ratione effutiat ore,   910
aurea tum dicat per terras flumina vulgo
fluxisse et gemmis florere arbusta suesse
aut hominem tanto membrorum esse impete natum,
trans maria alta pedum nisus ut ponere posset
et manibus totum circum se vertere caelum.   915
nam quod multa fuere in terris semina rerum
tempore quo primum tellus animalia fudit,
nil tamen est signi mixtas potuisse creari
inter se pecudes compactaque membra animantum,
propterea quia quae de terris nunc quoque abundant   920
herbarum genera ac fruges arbustaque laeta
non tamen inter se possunt complexa creari,
sed res quaeque suo ritu procedit et omnes
foedere naturae certo discrimina servant.

*In the days of old men were hardier than they are now. Their
food was the natural produce of the earth, their drink was the
running stream. They had neither fire nor clothing and lived
lawless lives. Life was full of the terrors of the unknown for
them: as yet they were not confident of the superiority of man
over beast.*

At genus humanum multo fuit illud in arvis   925
durius, ut decuit, tellus quod dura creasset,
et maioribus et solidis magis ossibus intus
fundatum, validis aptum per viscera nervis,

nec facile ex aestu nec frigore quod caperetur
nec novitate cibi nec labi corporis ulla.   930
multaque per caelum solis volventia lustra
vulgivago vitam traetabant more ferarum.
nec robustus erat curvi moderator aratri
quisquam, nec scibat ferro molirier arva
nec nova defodere in terram virgulta neque altis   935
arboribus veteres decidere falcibu' ramos.
quod sol atque imbres dederant, quod terra crearat
sponte sua, satis id placabat pectora donum.
glandiferas inter curabant corpora quercus
plerumque; et quae nunc hiberno tempore cernis   940
arbuta puniceo fieri matura colore,
plurima tum tellus etiam maiora ferebat.
multaque praeterea novitas tum florida mundi
pabula dura tulit, miseris mortalibus ampla.
at sedare sitim fluvii fontesque vocabant,   945
ut nunc montibus e magnis decursus aquai
claru' citat late sitientia saecla ferarum.
denique nota vagi silvestria templa tenebant
nympharum, quibus e scibant umori' fluenta
lubrica proluvie larga lavere umida saxa,   950
umida saxa, super viridi stillantia musco,
et partim plano scatere atque erumpere campo.
necdum res igni scibant tractare neque uti
pellibus et spoliis corpus vestire ferarum,
sed nemora atque cavos montis silvasque colebant 955
et frutices inter condebant squalida membra
verbera ventorum vitare imbrisque coacti.
nec commune bonum poterant spectare neque ullis
moribus inter se scibant nec legibus uti.
quod cuique obtulerat praedae fortuna, ferebat   960
sponte sua sibi quisque valere et vivere doctus.
et Venus in silvis iungebat corpora amantum;
conciliabat enim vel mutua quamque cupido

vel violenta viri vis atque impensa libido
vel pretium, glandes atque arbuta vel pira lecta.   965
et manuum mira freti virtute pedumque
consectabantur silvestria saecla ferarum
missilibus saxis et magno pondere clavae ;
multaque vincebant, vitabant pauca latebris ;
saetigerisque pares subus silvestria membra   970
nuda dabant terrae nocturno tempore capti,
circum se foliis ac frondibus involventes.
nec plangore diem magno solemque per agros
quaerebant pavidi palantes noctis in umbris,
sed taciti respectabant somnoque sepulti,   975
dum rosea face sol inferret lumina caelo.
a parvis quod enim consuerant cernere semper
alterno tenebras et lucem tempore gigni,
non erat ut fieri possent mirarier umquam
nec diffidere ne terras aeterna teneret   980
nox in perpetuum detracto lumine solis.
sed magis illud erat curae, quod saecla ferarum
infestam miseris faciebant saepe quietem.
eiectique domo fugiebant saxea tecta
spumigeri suis adventu validique leonis   985
atque intempesta cedebant nocte paventes
hospitibus saevis instrata cubilia fronde.

*And yet death was not more frequent then than now, for
though many were killed and devoured by wild beasts, and others
perished from hunger or from eating poisonous fruits, yet far
greater numbers are slain now in a single battle, or are wrecked
on voyages, while some eat themselves to death or are poisoned.*

Nec nimio tum plus quam nunc mortalia saecla
dulcia linquebant lamentis lumina vitae.
unus enim tum quisque magis deprensus eorum   990
pabula viva feris praebebat, dentibus haustus,
et nemora ac montis gemitu silvasque replebat

viva videns vivo sepeliri viscera busto.
et quos effugium servarat corpore adeso,
posterius tremulas super ulcera taetra tenentes 995
palmas horriferis accibant vocibus Orcum,
donec eos vita privarant vermina saeva
expertis opis, ignaros quid vulnera vellent.
at non multa virum sub signis milia ducta
una dies dabat exitio nec turbida ponti 1000
aequora lidebant navis ad saxa virosque.
hic temere incassum frustra mare saepe coortum
saevibat leviterque minas ponebat inanis,
nec poterat quemquam placidi pellacia ponti
subdola pellicere in fraudem ridentibus undis, 1005
improba navigiis ratio cum caeca iacebat.
tum penuria deinde cibi languentia leto
membra dabat, contra nunc rerum copia mersat.
illi imprudentes ipsi sibi saepe venenum
vergebant, nunc dant ⟨aliis⟩ sollertius ipsi. 1010

Soon followed the beginnings of civilization and family life,
which, coupled with the discovery of fire, gradually enervated
them. Love began to play its part, first between man and woman,
then between parents and children, presently between neigh-
bours, finally among nations.

Inde casas postquam ac pellis ignemque pararunt,
et mulier coniuncta viro concessit in unum
hospitium, ac lecti socialia iura duobus
cognita sunt, prolemque ex se videre creatam,
tum genus humanum primum mollescere coepit.
ignis enim curavit ut alsia corpora frigus 1015
non ita iam possent caeli sub tegmine ferre,
et Venus imminuit viris puerique parentum
blanditiis facile ingenium fregere superbum.
tunc et amicitiem coeperunt iungere aventes
finitimi inter se nec laedere nec violari, 1020
et pueros commendarunt muliebreque saeclum,

16

vocibus et gestu cum balbe significarent
imbecillorum esse aequum misererier omnis.
nec tamen omnimodis poterat concordia gigni,
sed bona magnaque pars servabat foedera caste ;   1025
aut genus humanum iam tum foret omne peremptum
nec potuisset adhuc perducere saecla propago.

*The gradual growth of language is like the instinctive actions
of young animals. One man could not have invented language
by himself : it was the slowly developed outcome of the natural
sounds and cries of man, even as animals also express different
emotions by different sounds.*

At varios linguae sonitus natura subegit
mittere et utilitas expressit nomina rerum,
non alia longe ratione atque ipsa videtur   1030
protrahere ad gestum pueros infantia linguae,
cum facit ut digito quae sint praesentia monstrent.
sentit enim vis quisque suas quoad possit abuti.
cornua nata prius vitulo quam frontibus exstent,
illis iratus petit atque infestus inurget.   1035
at catuli pantherarum scymnique leonum
unguibus ac pedibus iam tum morsuque repugnant,
vix etiam cum sunt dentes unguesque creati.
alituum porro genus alis omne videmus
fidere et a pinnis tremulum petere auxiliatum.   1040
proinde putare aliquem tum nomina distribuisse
rebus et inde homines didicisse vocabula prima,
desiperest. nam cur hic posset cuncta notare
vocibus et varios sonitus emittere linguae,
tempore eodem alii facere id non quisse putentur ?   1045
praeterea si non alii quoque vocibus usi
inter se fuerant, unde insita notities est
utilitatis et unde data est huic prima potestas,
quid vellet facere ut sciret animoque videret ?
cogere item pluris unus victosque domare   1050
non poterat, rerum ut perdiscere nomina vellent.

nec ratione docere ulla suadereque surdis,
quid sit opus facto, facilest; neque enim paterentur
nec ratione ulla sibi ferrent amplius auris
vocis inauditos sonitus obtundere frustra.   1055
postremo quid in hac mirabile tantoperest re,
si genus humanum, cui vox et lingua vigeret,
pro vario sensu varia res voce notaret?
cum pecudes mutae, cum denique saecla ferarum
dissimilis soleant voces variasque ciere,   1060
cum metus aut dolor est et cum iam gaudia gliscunt.
quippe etenim licet id rebus cognoscere apertis.
irritata canum cum primum magna Molossum
mollia ricta fremunt duros nudantia dentis,
longe alio sonitu rabie restricta minantur,   1065
et cum iam latrant et vocibus omnia complent.
et catulos blande cum lingua lambere temptant
aut ubi eos iactant pedibus morsuque petentes
suspensis teneros imitantur dentibus haustus,
longe alio pacto gannitu vocis adulant,   1070
et cum deserti baubantur in aedibus aut cum
plorantes fugiunt summisso corpore plagas.
denique non hinnitus item differre videtur,
inter equas ubi equus florenti aetate iuvencus
pinnigeri saevit calcaribus ictus amoris   1075
et fremitum patulis sub naribus edit ad arma,
et cum sic alias concussis artubus hinnit?
postremo genus alituum variaeque volucres,
accipitres atque ossifragae mergique marinis
fluctibus in salso victum vitamque petentes,   1080
longe alias alio iaciunt in tempore voces,
et cum de victu certant praedaeque repugnant.
et partim mutant cum tempestatibus una
raucisonos cantus, cornicum ut saecla vetusta
corvorumque greges ubi aquam dicuntur et imbris   1085
poscere et interdum ventos aurasque vocare.

ergo si varii sensus animalia cogunt,
muta tamen cum sint, varias emittere voces,
quanto mortalis magis aequumst tum potuisse
dissimilis alia atque alia res voce notare!   1090

*Lightning, or possibly the friction of branches in the first
instance, gave or suggested to men the use of fire. The sun
itself by its ripening action on fruit and corn would lead men by
analogy to cook their food.*

Illud in his rebus tacitus ne forte requiras,
fulmen detulit in terram mortalibus ignem
primitus, inde omnis flammarum diditur ardor.
multa videmus enim caelestibus inlita flammis
fulgere, cum caeli donavit plaga vapore.   1095
et ramosa tamen cum ventis pulsa vacillans
aestuat in ramos incumbens arboris arbor,
exprimitur validis extritus viribus ignis
et micat interdum flammai fervidus ardor,
mutua dum inter se rami stirpesque teruntur.   1100
quorum utrumque dedisse potest mortalibus ignem.
inde cibum coquere ac flammae mollire vapore
sol docuit, quoniam mitescere multa videbant
verberibus radiorum atque aestu victa per agros.

*Men with original ideas gradually raised mankind to the
higher civilization of combined life and property. At first the
merit of beauty, strength, and intellect had great weight, but
gradually the power of wealth became pre-eminent; the growth of
ambition was often ruinous to its victims, who for their folly
and greed well deserved the destruction with which Retribution
often visited them.*

Inque dies magis hi victum vitamque priorem   1105
commutare novis monstrabant rebu' benigni,
ingenio qui praestabant et corde vigebant.
condere coeperunt urbis arcemque locare
praesidium reges ipsi sibi perfugiumque,
et pecus atque agros divisere atque dedere   1110
pro facie cuiusque et viribus ingenioque;

nam facies multum valuit viresque vigebant.
posterius res inventast aurumque repertum,
quod facile et validis et pulchris dempsit honorem ;
divitioris enim sectam plerumque sequuntur   1115
quamlibet et fortes et pulchro corpore creti.
quod siquis vera vitam ratione gubernet,
divitiae grandes homini sunt vivere parce
aequo animo ; neque enim est umquam penuria parvi.
at claros homines voluerunt se atque potentis,   1120
ut fundamento stabili fortuna maneret
et placidam possent opulenti degere vitam,
nequiquam, quoniam ad summum succedere honorem
certantes iter infestum fecere viai,
et tamen e summo, quasi fulmen, deicit ictos   1125
invidia interdum contemptim in Tartara taetra ;
invidia quoniam, ceu fulmine, summa vaporant
plerumque et quae sunt aliis magis edita cumque ;
ut satius multo iam sit parere quietum
quam regere imperio res velle et regna tenere.   1130
proinde sine incassum defessi sanguine sudent,
angustum per iter luctantes ambitionis ;
quandoquidem sapiunt alieno ex ore petuntque
res ex auditis potius quam sensibus ipsis,
nec magis id nunc est neque erit mox quam fuit ante.   1135

Monarchy was overthrown and anarchy ensued, until self-interest taught man to appoint authorities responsible for the maintenance of law and order and for the suppressions of crime and blood-feuds. And now even if a man may occasionally escape punishment, he cannot avoid the stings of his own conscience.

Ergo regibus occisis subversa iacebat
pristina maiestas soliorum et sceptra superba,
et capitis summi praeclarum insigne cruentum
sub pedibus vulgi magnum lugebat honorem ;
nam cupide conculcatur nimis ante metutum.   1140
res itaque ad summam faecem turbasque redibat,

imperium sibi cum ac summatum quisque petebat.
inde magistratum partim docuere creare
iuraque constituere, ut vellent legibus uti.
nam genus humanum, defessum vi colere aevum,   1145
ex inimicitiis languebat ; quo magis ipsum
sponte sua cecidit sub leges artaque iura.
acrius ex ira quod enim se quisque parabat
ulcisci quam nunc concessumst legibus aequis,
hanc ob rem est homines pertaesum vi colere aevum.   1150
inde metus maculat poenarum praemia vitae.
circumretit enim vis atque iniuria quemque
atque, unde exortast, ad eum plerumque revertit,
nec facilest placidam ac pacatam degere vitam
qui violat factis communia foedera pacis.   1155
etsi fallit enim divum genus humanumque,
perpetuo tamen id fore clam diffidere debet ;
quippe ubi se multi per somnia saepe loquentes
aut morbo delirantes protraxe ferantur
et celata ⟨diu⟩ in medium peccata dedisse.   1160

*The beginnings of religion. Visions and dreams first planted
in man a belief in the existence of gods. And the immutable
appearance of these visions would give rise to the belief in the
immortality of deities. Again the unaccountable changes of
seasons and celestial phenomena would naturally result in the
sky being assigned to the gods as their especial province or
sphere of action and consequently as their home.*

Nunc quae causa deum per magnas numina gentis
pervulgarit et ararum compleverit urbis
suscipiendaque curarit sollemnia sacra,
quae nunc in magnis florent sacra rebu' locisque,
unde etiam nunc est mortalibus insitus horror   1165
qui delubra deum nova toto suscitat orbi
terrarum et festis cogit celebrare diebus,
non ita difficilest rationem reddere verbis.
quippe etenim iam tum divum mortalia saecla
egregias animo facies vigilante videbant   1170

et magis in somnis mirando corporis auctu.
his igitur sensum tribuebant propterea quod
membra movere videbantur vocesque superbas
mittere pro facie praeclara et viribus amplis.
aeternamque dabant vitam, quia semper eorum   1175
suppeditabatur facies et forma manebat,
et tamen omnino quod tantis viribus auctos
non temere ulla vi convinci posse putabant.
fortunisque ideo longe praestare putabant,
quod mortis timor haud quemquam vexaret eorum,   1180
et simul in somnis quia multa et mira videbant
efficere et nullum capere ipsos inde laborem.
praeterea caeli rationes ordine certo
et varia annorum cernebant tempora verti
nec poterant quibus id fieret cognoscere causis.   1185
ergo perfugium sibi habebant omnia divis
tradere et illorum nutu facere omnia flecti.
in caeloque deum sedis et templa locarunt,
per caelum volvi quia sol et luna videtur,
luna dies et nox et noctis signa severa   1190
noctivagaeque faces caeli flammaeque volantes,
nubila sol imbres nix venti fulmina grando
et rapidi fremitus et murmura magna minarum.

*Men have courted misery by assigning to the gods not only
supernatural powers but also the capricious use of them. The
truly pious man is not the superstitious man, but rather he
whose conscience is at rest. The vastness of the universe fills us
with alarm, thunder terrifies us lest it be the harbinger of
divine vengeance on our crimes. The mighty strength of the
sea, of the wind and of earthquakes naturally instil into men's
minds a heartful realization of their own insignificance.*

O genus infelix humanum, talia divis
cum tribuit facta atque iras adiunxit acerbas!   1195
quantos tum gemitus ipsi sibi, quantaque nobis
vulnera, quas lacrimas peperere minoribu' nostris!
nec pietas ullast velatum saepe videri

vertier ad lapidem atque omnis accedere ad aras
nec procumbere humi prostratum et pandere palmas 1200
ante deum delubra nec aras sanguine multo
spargere quadrupedum nec votis nectere vota,
sed mage pacata posse omnia mente tueri.
nam cum suspicimus magni caelestia mundi
templa super stellisque micantibus aethera fixum, 1205
et venit in mentem solis lunaeque viarum,
tunc aliis oppressa malis in pectora cura
illa quoque expergefactum caput erigere infit,
nequae forte deum nobis immensa potestas
sit, vario motu quae candida sidera verset. 1210
temptat enim dubiam mentem rationis egestas,
ecquaenam fuerit mundi genitalis origo,
et simul ecquae sit finis, quoad moenia mundi
solliciti motus hunc possint ferre laborem,
an divinitus aeterna donata salute 1215
perpetuo possint aevi labentia tractu
immensi validas aevi contemnere viris.
praeterea cui non animus formidine divum
contrahitur, cui non correpunt membra pavore,
fulminis horribili cum plaga torrida tellus 1220
contremit et magnum percurrunt murmura caelum?
non populi gentesque tremunt, regesque superbi
corripiunt divum percussi membra timore,
nequid ob admissum foede dictumve superbe
poenarum grave sit solvendi tempus adultum? 1225
summa etiam cum vis violenti per mare venti
induperatorem classis super aequora verrit
cum validis pariter legionibus atque elephantis,
non divum pacem votis adit ac prece quaesit
ventorum pavidus paces animasque secundas, 1230
nequiquam, quoniam violento turbine saepe
correptus nilo fertur minus ad vada leti?
usque adeo res humanas vis abdita quaedam

obterit et pulchros fascis saevasque securis
proculcare ac ludibrio sibi habere videtur.   1235
denique sub pedibus tellus cum tota vacillat
concussaeque cadunt urbes dubiaeque minantur,
quid mirum si se temnunt mortalia saecla
atque potestates magnas mirasque relinquunt
in rebus viris divum, quae cuncta gubernent?   1240

*Then followed the discovery of metals by the heating of the earth
from forest fires kindled by lightning or by man's agency. The
metals congealed and attracted men first by their beauty, then by
their utility. They learned to fuse them and beat them into
shape, at first for use in ordinary life. Originally copper was
valued more highly than gold or silver: gradually gold won
the premier position: even so does the wheel of Fortune make
all things change from prosperity to adversity and from adversity to prosperity.*

Quod superest, aes atque aurum ferrumque repertumst
et simul argenti pondus plumbique potestas,
ignis ubi ingentis silvas ardore cremarat
montibus in magnis, seu caeli fulmine misso,
sive quod inter se bellum silvestre gerentes   1245
hostibus intulerant ignem formidinis ergo,
sive quod inducti terrae bonitate volebant
pandere agros pinguis et pascua reddere rura,
sive feras interficere et ditescere praeda.
nam fovea atque igni prius est venarier ortum   1250
quam saepire plagis saltum canibusque ciere.
quidquid id est, quacumque e causa flammeus ardor
horribili sonitu silvas exederat altis
ab radicibus et terram percoxerat igni,
manabat venis ferventibus in loca terrae   1255
concava conveniens argenti rivus et auri,
aeris item et plumbi. quae cum concreta videbant
posterius claro in terra splendere colore,
tollebant nitido capti levique lepore,
et simili formata videbant esse figura   1260

24

atque lacunarum fuerant vestigia cuique.
tum penetrabat eos posse haec liquefacta calore
quamlibet in formam et faciem decurrere rerum
et prorsum quamvis in acuta ac tenvia posse
mucronum duci fastigia procudendo,   1265
ut sibi tela parent, silvasque ut caedere possint
materiemque dolare et levia radere tigna
et terebrare etiam ac pertundere perque forare.
nec minus argento facere haec auroque parabant
quam validi primum violentis viribus aeris,   1270
nequiquam, quoniam cedebat victa potestas,
nec poterant pariter durum sufferre laborem.
tum fuit in pretio magis aes aurumque iacebat
propter inutilitatem hebeti mucrone retusum.
nunc iacet aes, aurum in summum successit honorem.   1275
sic volvenda aetas commutat tempora rerum.
quod fuit in pretio, fit nullo denique honore;
porro aliud succedit et ⟨e⟩ contemptibus exit
inque dies magis appetitur floretque repertum
laudibus et miro est mortalis inter honore.   1280

*The earliest arms were the natural weapons of nails, teeth,
&c., then stones and clubs and fire : later came bronze weapons,
until at last iron prevailed. Soon the horse was ridden into
battle, then came chariots with two horses, later with four. At
last the strength of trained elephants was employed in warfare :
new death-dealing contrivances were continually being invented.*

Nunc tibi quo pacto ferri natura reperta
sit facilest ipsi per te cognoscere, Memmi.
arma antiqua manus ungues dentesque fuerunt
et lapides et item silvarum fragmina rami,
et flamma atque ignes, postquam sunt cognita primum. 1285
posterius ferri vis est aerisque reperta.
et prior aeris erat quam ferri cognitus usus,
quo facilis magis est natura et copia maior.
aere solum terrae tractabant, aereque belli

miscebant fluctus et vulnera vasta serebant 1290
et pecus atque agros adimebant. nam facile ollis
omnia cedebant armatis nuda et inerma.
inde minutatim processit ferreus ensis
versaque in opprobrium species est falcis aenae,
et ferro coepere solum proscindere terrae 1295
exaequataque sunt creperi certamina belli.
et prius est armatum in equi conscendere costas
et moderarier hunc frenis dextraque vigere
quam biiugo curru belli temptare pericla.
et biiugos prius est quam bis coniungere binos 1300
et quam falciferos armatum escendere currus.
inde boves lucas turrito corpore, taetras,
anguimanus, belli docuerunt vulnera Poeni
sufferre et magnas Martis turbare catervas.
sic alid ex alio peperit discordia tristis, 1305
horribile humanis quod gentibus esset in armis,
inque dies belli terroribus addidit augmen.

*All sorts of wild animals were trained for war, but the
attempts were unsuccessful, as the beasts made no distinction
between friend and foe in the fury of the fray. Finally only
when in despair the weaker had recourse to such allies.*

Temptarunt etiam tauros in moenere belli
expertique sues saevos sunt mittere in hostis.
et validos partim prae se misere leones 1310
cum doctoribus armatis saevisque magistris
qui moderarier his possent vinclisque tenere,
nequiquam, quoniam permixta caede calentes
turbabant saevi nullo discrimine turmas,
terrificas capitum quatientes undique cristas, 1315
nec poterant equites fremitu perterrita equorum
pectora mulcere et frenis convertere in hostis.
irritata leae iaciebant corpora saltu
undique et adversum venientibus ora petebant
et nec opinantis a tergo deripiebant 1320

deplexaeque dabant in terram vulnere victos,
morsibus adfixae validis atque unguibus uncis.
iactabantque suos tauri pedibusque terebant
et latera ac ventris hauribant subter equorum
cornibus et terram minitanti fronte ruebant.   1325
et validis socios caedebant dentibus apri
tela infracta suo tingentes sanguine saevi,
permixtasque dabant equitum peditumque ruinas.   1329
nam transversa feros exibant dentis adactus   1330
iumenta aut pedibus ventos erecta petebant,
nequiquam, quoniam ab nervis succisa videres
concidere atque gravi terram consternere casu.
siquos ante domi domitos satis esse putabant,
effervescere cernebant in rebus agendis   1335
vulneribus clamore fuga terrore tumultu,
nec poterant ullam partem reducere eorum ;
diffugiebat enim varium genus omne ferarum ;
ut nunc saepe boves lucae ferro male mactae
diffugiunt, fera fata suis cum multa dedere.   1340
sed facere id non tam vincendi spe voluerunt,   1347
quam dare quod gemerent hostes, ipsique perire,
qui numero diffidebant armisque vacabant.

The invention of weaving followed the discovery of iron,
which was used for making the necessary instruments. At first
men did the weaving, till the scoffs of the farmers drove them to
resign such work to women.

Nexilis ante fuit vestis quam textile tegmen.   1350
textile post ferrumst, quia ferro tela paratur,
nec ratione alia possunt tam levia gigni
insilia ac fusi radii scapique sonantes.
et facere ante viros lanam natura coegit
quam muliebre genus ; nam longe praestat in arte   1355
et sollertius est multo genus omne virile ;
agricolae donec vitio vertere severi,
ut muliebribus id manibus concedere vellent

atque ipsi pariter durum sufferre laborem
atque opere in duro durarent membra manusque.　　1360

*Nature was the chief instructress of man in agriculture. By
observation man learned how to sow seeds and to graft and
cultivate the land, until the present high perfection of farming
has been attained.*

At specimen sationis et insitionis origo
ipsa fuit rerum primum natura creatrix,
arboribus quoniam bacae glandesque caducae
tempestiva dabant pullorum examina subter ;
unde etiam libitumst stirpis committere ramis　　1365
et nova defodere in terram virgulta per agros.
inde aliam atque aliam culturam dulcis agelli
temptabant fructusque feros mansuescere terram
cernebant indulgendo blandeque colendo.
inque dies magis in montem succedere silvas　　1370
cogebant infraque locum concedere cultis,
prata lacus rivos segetes vinetaque laeta
collibus et campis ut haberent, atque olearum
caerula distingũens inter plaga currere posset
per tumulos et convallis camposque profusa ;　　1375
ut nunc esse vides vario distincta lepore
omnia, quae pomis intersita dulcibus ornant
arbustisque tenent felicibus obsita circum.

*So too man learnt singing from birds, reed- and later flute-
playing from hearing the winds blow through reed beds. Music
was especially popular in the country and at the rustic festivals,
and rough though it would seem to us, it gave the peasants
great pleasure. Life became less simple, luxury crept in : men
learned to despise acorns as food and skins of beasts as clothing :
now they struggle to deck themselves with purple and gold, and
allow greed of gain and ambition to mar the natural happiness
of life.*

At liquidas avium voces imitarier ore
ante fuit multo quam levia carmina cantu　　1380
concelebrare homines possent aurisque iuvare.

et zephyri, cava per calamorum, sibila primum
agrestis docuere cavas inflare cicutas.
inde minutatim dulcis didicere querelas,
tibia quas fundit digitis pulsata canentum,   1385
avia per nemora ac silvas saltusque repertas,
per loca pastorum deserta atque otia dia.
haec animos ollis mulcebant atque iuvabant   1390
cum satiate cibi; nam tum sunt omnia cordi.
saepe itaque inter se prostrati in gramine molli
propter aquae rivum sub ramis arboris altae
non magnis opibus iucunde corpora habebant,
praesertim cum tempestas ridebat et anni   1395
tempora pingebant viridantis floribus herbas.
tum ioca, tum sermo, tum dulces esse cachinni
consuerant. agrestis enim tum musa vigebat;
tum caput atque umeros plexis redimire coronis
floribus et foliis lascivia laeta monebat,   1400
atque extra numerum procedere membra moventis
duriter et duro terram pede pellere matrem;
unde oriebantur risus dulcesque cachinni,
omnia quod nova tum magis haec et mira vigebant.
et vigilantibus hinc aderant solacia somni,   1405
ducere multimodis voces et flectere cantus
et supera calamos unco percurrere labro;
unde etiam vigiles nunc haec accepta tuentur
et numerum servare recens didicere, neque hilo
maiorem interea capiunt dulcedini' fructum   1410
quam silvestre genus capiebat terrigenarum.
nam quod adest praesto, nisi quid cognovimus ante
suavius, in primis placet et pollere videtur,
posteriorque fere melior res illa reperta
perdit et immutat sensus ad pristina quaeque.   1415
sic odium coepit glandis, sic illa relicta
strata cubilia sunt herbis et frondibus aucta.
pellis item cecidit vestis contempta ferinae;

29

quam reor invidia tali tunc esse repertam,
ut letum insidiis qui gessit primus obiret,   1420
et tamen inter eos distractam sanguine multo
disperiisse neque in fructum convertere quisse.
tunc igitur pelles, nunc aurum et purpura curis
exercent hominum vitam belloque fatigant;
quo magis in nobis, ut opinor, culpa resedit.   1425
frigus enim nudos sine pellibus excruciabat
terrigenas; at nos nil laedit veste carere
purpurea atque auro signisque ingentibus apta,
dum plebeia tamen sit quae defendere possit.
ergo hominum genus incassum frustraque laborat   1430
semper et in curis consumit inanibus aevum,
nimirum quia non cognovit quae sit habendi
finis et omnino quoad crescat vera voluptas.
idque minutatim vitam provexit in altum
et belli magnos commovit funditus aestus.   1435

*Gradually men learned to anticipate the seasons of the year by
watching the motions of the sun and moon.*

At vigiles mundi magnum versatile templum
sol et luna suo lustrantes lumine circum
perdocuere homines annorum tempora verti
et certa ratione geri rem atque ordine certo.

*Men gradually learned the value of social life in towns and
lands were allotted to individuals. Similar influences developed
the growth of alliance between cities. The inventive power of
man now devised ships and navigation, the alphabet and
literature.*

Iam validis saepti degebant turribus aevum   1440
et divisa colebatur discretaque tellus,
iam mare velivolis florebat puppibus; urbes
auxilia ac socios iam pacto foedere habebant,
carminibus cum res gestas coepere poetae
tradere; nec multo priu' sunt elementa reperta.   1445

propterea quid sit prius actum respicere aetas
nostra nequit, nisi qua ratio vestigia monstrat.

*Man by gradual experience has evolved various useful arts,
and later many kinds of luxury, maintaining a steady if slow
progress to full development, and finally reaching the perfection
of the present time.*

Navigia atque agri culturas moenia leges
arma vias vestis et cetera de genere horum,
praemia, delicias quoque vitae funditus omnis,   1450
carmina picturas, et daedala signa polire,
usus et impigrae simul experientia mentis
paulatim docuit pedetemptim progredientis.
sic unumquicquid paulatim protrahit aetas
in medium ratioque in luminis erigit oras.   1455
namque alid ex alio clarescere cordi' videbant
artibus, ad summum donec venere cacumen.

NOTES

783. principio, 'at the beginning of the world.' The account of the creation of the world in the first chapter of Genesis may be compared with this passage. The straightforward simplicity of both accounts and the harmony of the biblical and pagan narratives are remarkable. The early philosophers agreed that primarily all living things sprang from the earth. Similar descriptions of the creation are found at the beginning of the first book of Ovid's *Metamorphoses* and in Hesiod's *Works and Days*.

786. arboribus. Wakefield quotes Empedocles' theory that herbage was created first, πρῶτα τῶν ζῴων τὰ δένδρα ἐκ γῆς ἀναδῦναι. *certamen* is the subject to *datumst*.

787. magnum certamen, 'a keen rivalry.'

immissis habenis, 'in unchecked profusion': a somewhat incongruous metaphor for the riotous luxuriance of thick jungle growth. Vergil, however, has no hesitation in using the phrase in a similar context, where he describes the vine shoot as growing freely: *Georg*. ii. 364 'palmes se agit laxis immissus habenis'.

788. primum. Munro says that as birds have rudiments of feathers and animals have hair at birth and before they show any activity in life, so the earth at creation had herbage before it produced animate beings: Ov. *Met*. i. 44 'iussit fronde tegi silvas'.

789. pennipotentum: a word coined by Lucretius, found only here and in ii. 878.

791. inde loci: so too in l. 443; cf. l. 807 *ubi loci*, a partitive genitive; cf. *postea loci*, 'afterwards.'

mortalia saecla, 'all living creatures,' the generations of living creatures that must die.

792. multa modis multis. Notice the alliteration; see Introduction, The Style of Lucretius. Observe that Lucretius has no objection to the repetition of meaning in different words; cf. l. 801, l. 1002 'temere incassum frustra', l. 1050. Here *modis multis = varia ratione*.

793. de caelo. Cf. ii. 1153 'haud mortalia saecla superne aurea de caelo demisit funis in arva': the Stoics maintaining that life came from heaven let down by a golden cord. Lucretius denies that the gods had any interest or share in the creation of the world.

794. de salsis lacunis = *mare*; cf. ii. 1155 'nec mare nec fluctus plangentes saxa crearunt, sed genuit tellus eadem quae nunc alit ex se': Lucretius says that life could not be generated in the first instance in the sea, but required the warmth and nurturing care of mother earth.

795. linquitur. We find this impersonal use of *linquitur* with *ut* and the subj. in ii. 914. Lucretius uses impersonal verbs frequently, *convenit, penetrabat, superest, sequitur.* Out of the four elements Lucretius has dismissed the claims of fire, air, and water to be the creative power, therefore earth alone remains as the universal mother.

797. **exsistunt** = *exoriuntur* : it is usually constructed with *ex* or *ab,* and not with the simple ablative as here.

798. **concreta,** 'are moulded into shape'; so l. 1257. In l. 1116 we have the uncompounded verb *creti.* So in Cic. *Tusc.* v. 24. 69 'initia unde essent omnia orta, generata, concreta'.

799. **minus** with *mirum,* not with *quo.*

800. **nova** : when the productive powers of the earth were still vigorous ; cf. l. 907 'tellure nova caeloque recenti'.

adulta is in agreement with *plura.*

801. **alituum.** This form of the genit. plur. of *ales,* which is convenient for scansion, is found not only in Lucretius but also in Verg. *Aen.* viii. 27 and other poets.

variae=l. 825 'volucris variantibu' formis'.

802. **ova relinquebant exclusae** : i. e. were hatched. Ov. *Met.* i. 75 'cepit volucris agitabilis aer'. Cicero uses *excludere* frequently in this sense. Verg. *Georg.* ii. 338 'ver illud erat ... et hibernis parcebant flatibus Euri, cum primae lucem pecudes hausere,' where the sense is the same.

803. **folliculos** : little leathern bags, here 'eggs'. Duff compares iv. 58 'teretes ponunt tunicas aestate cicadae'.

805. **tibi** = τοι, 'let me tell you': ethic dative: cf. l. 1209 *nobis.*

mortalia saecla, 'races of men,' but see l. 791.

806. **calor atque umor** are the two great essentials of production and growth.

807. **hoc,** 'therefore.'

ubi loci : see l. 791.

808. **terram apti,** 'embracing,' 'clinging to,' from *apiscor.* Plaut. *Capt.* iv. 1. 8 'hereditatem sum aptus'.

809. **aetas**: the age of the growing infant. MSS. have *aestas,* the warmth of the growing child. Others read *aestus,* the restless movements of the infants and the resulting heat.

810. **petessens** : an old desiderative form : note the transference of *fugiens* and *petessens* to *aetas* from *infantum,* to which the two participles properly belong.

811. **ibi** : for *illic,* i. e. *ad uteros,* 'turned the pores of the earth in that direction,' causing the flow of nutriment to the necessary places.

812. **cogebat** : the object is *foramina* : **sucum** is the object of *fundere.*

813. **consimilem** : with genitive : so too in l. 714; more usually it is constructed with the dative.

815. **impetus ille alimenti,** 'that stream,' or 'rush of nourishment,' which served to feed the child while still unborn.

816. **vapor** : the temperate warmth of the earth in the early days rendering clothing unnecessary ; cf. ll. 818-9.

817. **lanugine** is the soft, velvety growth of luxuriant grass.

818. **novitas.** See on *nova*, l. 800, and on *ova*, l. 802.

820. As the world grew and developed, so also did the extremes of heat and cold gradually become more marked.

821-2. Cf. 795-6.

821. **etiam atque etiam** : understand *tibi*, ' let me tell you again and again.'

823. **humanum.** Ovid said that creation found its consummation in the birth of man. *Met.* i. 76 ' sanctius his animal mentisque capacius altae deerat adhuc, et quod dominari in cetera posset : natus homo est '.

animal : here only in Lucretius in the singular.

prope certo tempore. Cf. Verg. *Georg.* ii. 338, quoted in note on *ova*, l. 802.

fudit expresses well the generous productiveness of nature. Verg. *Georg.* i. 13 ' fudit equum tellus '.

824. **montibu'.** A favourite suppression of final *s* in Lucretius : the usage is common also in the earlier Latin poets : final *s*, especially in short syllables, was lightly sounded.

825. **variantibu'.** Cf. l. 801.

826. **finem :** usually masculine, but feminine in ante- and post-classical writers and in poets ; cf. ll. 1213, 1432. There is only one instance of the plural with a feminine adj. Varro *L. L.* v. i. 13.

827. **destitit.** Munro quotes ii. 1150 ' effetaque tellus vix animalia parva creat quae cuncta creavit saecla '.

spatio vetusto=*senectute*.

828-9. Cf. ll. 834-5.

829. **excipere,** ' to overtake.'

830. **manet,** ' remains unchanged.' Cf. l. 1176.

831. **vertere :** intransitive (cf. iv. 1130) for the more usual *se vertere* or *verti*. In l. 1422 *convertere* is used in the same way. Lucretius uses also as neuter verbs *volvo, traho, moveo, teneo, immuto*. For the substance of ll. 831-3 cf. ll. 1276-8.

832-3. The doctrine of *ἰσονομία*, the equilibrium or balance of the world, as held by Epicurus, appears here.

833. **porro,** ' forthwith,' ' and at once.'

contemptibus. Note the use of the plural as in l. 1278.

835. **alter :** for *alius* ; cf. l. 829.

836. The earth ceases its old functions and develops fresh ones more suitable to the needs and the progress of civilization, and so the equilibrium is maintained. Observe how similar this is to the opinions of modern science on the variations and extinction of certain species. With *possit* repeat *ut*.

838. **mira facie :** descriptive ablative.

839. **androgynum,** ' the man-woman,' a being combining the two sexes : the word is borrowed from the Greek, as also the synonym *hermaphroditus*. The Latin word is *semivir* or *semimas*.

interutrasque. So in l. 472, an adverb ; cf. *interea*. For the form of the termination Munro compares *alias* and *foras*. Note *interŭtrasque* followed by *ŭtrum, ŭtrimque*. Cf. ll. 1163-4 *săcra, săcra*, and note.

nec utrum=*neutrum* ; *nec* and *ne* were the old forms of the negative ; cf. *neglego, nec-lego*, not to regard, disregard.

840. **orba**: more commonly constructed with the ablative. Verg. *Georg.* iv. 309 'visenda modis animalia miris, trunca pedum primo'.

viduata: also far more usually constructed with the ablative ; cf. ii. 843 'corpora secreta teporis'; i. 1041 'materies aversa viai'.

vicissim=*contra*.

841. **vultu**=*luminibus, oculis*. Cf. Verg. *Aen.* xii. 70 'figitque in virgine vultus'. These monstrosities of nature still recur from time to time.

842. **adhaesus** is a Lucretian word.

844. **quod foret usus**. So in iv. 831 'quae foret usus': *quod* is accusative of reference (in place of the usual ablative) or else *sumere* is understood; Plaut. *Truc.* v. 10 'puero opus est cibum'. Cato *R. R.* 15 '(calcis) opus est unum modium '. Duff compares l. 1053 'quid sit opus facto,' 'in respect of what there is need of action.' MS. has 'quod volet usus'.

846. **absterruit**. So in iv. 1233 'nec divina satum genitalem numina cuiquam absterrent'=σοβεῖν, 'frighten away,' hence, 'remove.'

847. **cupitum aetatis florem**. Cf. iii. 770 'cupitum aetatis tangere florem'=*crescere*, i. e. they perished before reaching maturity. So in Greek we find in Pindar ἄωτος ζωᾶς, 'the flower or prime of life.'

848. **Veneris res**, 'union of love' or 'marriage.' The Romans were fond of using proper names instead of common nouns; cf. Ter. *Eun.* iv. 5. 6 'sine Cerere et Libero friget Venus', 'Love in a hut with water and a crust,' Keats. We find the same proverb in Cic. *N. D.* ii. 23. 60.

849. All conditions must be favourable to ensure procreation.

concurrere, 'happen at the same time,' 'meet together.'

debere is the only instance of hypermeter in Lucretius : it is not uncommon in Vergil, but is practically unknown in Greek hexameters.

850. Notice the strong alliteration : in l. 856 we find a more emphatic instance still. The first syllable of both the verb and the subst. *propago* is variable ; cf. l. 856.

procudere : i. e. to establish the continuity : the metaphor is from forging metal, 'to weld on the anvil of life the links of future generations.' Cf. Plaut. *Ps.* ii. 2. 20 'haec mihi incus est : procudam ego hodie hinc multos dolos'.

855. **tum** : in the old days when life was a struggle and only the best fitted survived, exactly as modern science teaches us.

animantum : all kinds of living creatures.

856. Cf. l. 850.

857. The old pronunciation of the Latin *v* as the English *w* would emphasize the alliteration of such lines as these. 'Drinking in the breath of life.' Verg. *Aen.* i. 546 'si vescitur aura aetheria'.

858. These three qualities represent the fox, the lion, and the deer mentioned in ll. 862–3.

aut denique, 'or even'; the adverb implies that this physical quality is a gift inferior to the two mental qualities. Take *est* with *tutata*.

859. **ex ineunte aevo**=a *primis annis*.

reservans, 'preserve,' i.e. keep back for something better than death.

860. Here the domestic animals which are mentioned in ll. 864-6 are meant, such as dogs, horses, sheep, and cattle.

862. **principio**, 'in the first place,' not as in l. 783.

saecla: sc. *animalium* not *hominum*. Verg. *Aen.* iv. 154 'atque agmina cervi pulverulenta fuga glomerant'.

864. **levisomna**: ἅπαξ λεγ. Cf. Hor. *Od.* iii. 16. 2 'vigilum canum tristes excubiae munierant'.

cum has the same force as the simple ablative and this use is common in Lucretius; cf. l. 904. Duff adds l. 352 'solido cum corpore'. He mentions also the instance in Homer of the faithful dog Argos, and remarks that Plato finds in the dog the qualities proper for the guardians of his ideal State. *Republ.* ii. 375, 376.

865. **veterino**: more fully in l. 890 'veterino semine equorum', horses : the word is contracted from *vehiterinus* from *veho*, a beast of burden, rather than a draught-animal.

866. **bucera**: from the Greek βούκερως: in ii. 663 we have 'buceriaeque greges'. Ov. *Met.* vi. 395 'lanigerosque greges armentaque bucera pavit'.

867. **Memmi**. Gaius Memmius was a Roman noble of distinguished birth: after holding the praetorship he served as propraetor of Bithynia. It was to this Memmius that Lucretius dedicated his poem.

868. **secuta**: in the sense of *consequor* or *peto*, it governs *pabula parta*.

869. **suo sine labore**: man supplies domestic animals with food prepared by his own labour in return for the labour and services performed by them.

871. **quis**: i.e. *animalia quibus*.

horum: i.e. no especial qualities to recommend them. The following lines illustrate Darwin's theory of the survival of the fittest.

872. **sponte sua**. So in ll. 938, 961 ; originally, 'of their own free will,' here, 'by their own efforts.' Plaut. *Truc.* ii. 6. 45 'nequeo pedibus mea sponte ambulare'.

873. **quare**=*quamobrem*: practically ablative of the cause.

874. **pasci**: as βόσκειν of maintaining inferiors or those unable to help themselves: of animals, slaves, and even of aged parents, whereas *alere*=τρέφειν is used in a more complimentary sense. Hor. *Sat.* i. 6. 103 'plures calones atque caballi pascendi'; Petron. 57 'viginti ventres pasco et canem'.

esseque. In Augustan poetry it was very exceptional to attach *que* or *ve* to a word ending in a short *e*: Lucretius, however, uses it frequently: l. 1021 *muliebreque*, l. 1052 *suadereque*, l. 1289 *aereque*.

875. **scilicet**: *scire licet* rather than *sci* (imperative) *licet*. See

Lindsay's *Short Historical Lat. Grammar*, p. 124. In meaning it is equivalent to δηλονότι, 'you must know.'

    aliis : *dativ. commodi.*

    praedae lucroque : predicat. dat.   See on l. 960.

876. **indupedita** : for *impedita*, as in i. 240, ii. 102, iv. 70. Lucretius has also *indugredi, induperator* l. 1227, and *indu*. In vi. 890 *endo mari* for *in mari* ; cf. ἔνδον.

    fatalibus vinclis, ' bonds of destiny,' i. e. theii natural dis advantages which hindered them in the struggle for existence.

878. **fuerunt** : to be scanned *fŭĕrŭnt* : the *e* of the third perfect plural is sometimes short in poetry ; cf. *dedĕrunt, stetĕrunt, tulĕrunt.*

879. **duplici natura** : descriptive ablative.

881. **potestas partis ut non par esse potissit**, ' so that the power in creatures born of two different species cannot be alike.' In the next few lines Lucretius' meaning becomes quite clear. We find *potesse* and *potis est* in Lucretius ; here we have the subjunctive.   See *possum, init*, Lewis and Short.

    hinc illinc : the two component parts or different natures.

    partis is the dative of the participle from *pario*.

882. **hinc**, ' from the following arguments.'   This line occurs in iv. 53.   Lucretius is here addressing not Memmius so much as any chance reader.

883. **principio**, ' to begin with.' *circum . . . actis*, tmesis is common in Lucretius, as in all early poets, also in Greek; cf. ll. 1128, 1268, 1374.   Cf. Butler's *Hudibras*, Pt. i, c. i, 328 'that old Pyg—(what d'ye call him) malion.   Hooker *Eccl. Polit.* v. ' creatures of what kind soever.'

885. **quaeret**, ' will cry out for.'   Ov. *Met.* vi. 342 'uberaque ebiberant avidi lactantia nati '.

886. **aetate senecta**: so in l. 896 the adjective is rare.   In iii. 772 ' membris exire senectis '.

888. **tum demum** : very emphatic, ' then, and not till then.'

    pueris : the dative of the party interested.

889. Cf. Verg. *Aen.* x. 324 'flaventem prima lanugine malas Clytium '.

890. **ne credas**: final not prohibitive ; cf. l. 1091.

    veterino semine.   Cf. l. 865.

    neque is more forcible than the simple conjunction *et*, as it recalls *ne credas* to the reader's mind.

892. **succinctas.**   Verg. *Ecl.* vi. 74 ' Scyllam . . . succinctam latrantibus monstris . . . nautas canibus lacerasse marinis '.   The Latin poets represent Scylla as more terrifying than the Scylla of Homer, *Od.* xii. 86–1co.

895. **sumunt**= *consequuntur*, ' reach their full bodily strength.' With **proiciunt** understand *robora*.

897. **Venere.**   Cf. l. 848=*stimulis amoris*.

    unis : we find the plural in iii. 616 'unis sedibus '.   Cic. *Flacc.* 63 ' unis moribus vivunt,' ' are endowed with similarity of habits.'

898. **neque sunt** : a second relative sentence parallel with **quae** neque . . . would have been more grammatical.

899. cicuta. iv. 640 'nobis veratrum est acre venenum, at capris adipes et coturnicibus auget'. One man's meat is another man's poison.

900. barbigeras. Cf. vi. 970 'barbigeras capellas'. The word is coined by and found only in Lucretius.

903. visceris, 'flesh,' all that lies between the skin and bones, so in ll. 928, 993. Translate in the following order 'visceris et sanguinis quodcumque in terris exstet'.

904. qui: old ablative = *quomodo*. For **triplici cum corpore** cf. l. 864.

905-6. This description is an exact imitation of a passage in Homer, *Il.* vi. 181-2 πρόσθε λέων, ὄπιθεν δὲ δράκων, μέσση δὲ χίμαιρα δεινὸν ἀποπνείουσα πυρὸς μένος αἰθομένοιο.

media ipsa, 'in the middle a goat, from which it receives its name:' note the full emphasis of ipsa.

foras: of motion outside, while *foris* is of rest outside ; the two, however, are frequently confused.

907. See l. 800 and note.

908. qui fingit: i. e. Empedocles who believed in the existence of bulls with men's heads and men with bulls' heads. Ov. *Ar. Am.* ii. 24 'semibovemque virum, semivirumque bovem'.

animalia: i. e. *monstra.*

910. licet: with subj. without *ut*, 'may babble out': *licet* must be repeated with *dicat* in the next line. In l. 792 we have 'varia ratione'.

911. aurea: to be taken predicatively : streams such as the river Pactolus in Lydia. Verg. *Aen.* x. 142 'Pactolus irrigat auro'. So too in *Georg.* ii. 165 'haec eadem argenti rivos aerisque metalla ostendit venis atque auro plurima fluxit'. The river Hermus had the same qualities. *Georg.* ii. 137 'auro turbidus Hermus'. See ll. 1255-6, which recall Milton, *Paradise Lost*, xi. 565 'Two massy clods of iron and brass Had melted, whether found where casual fire Had wasted woods on mountain or in vale, Down to the veins of earth, thence gliding hot To some cave's mouth.'

912. arbusta: for *arbores*, as *animantum* for *animalium*, for the sake of the metre. Cf. l. 1378.

suesse: for *suevisse* ; cf. l. 53 *suerit.* Perhaps the idea originated in the glistening of the morning dew on the leaves in the sunlight.

913. impete, 'size and strength' : more usually of strength alone. This word is used only in the genitive and ablative.

914. pedum nisus ponere, 'plant his footsteps firmly': contrast vi. 834 'pinnarum nisus inanis,' of the unsure flight of birds. For the idea of ll. 913-5 compare i. 199-201 'cur homines tantos natura parare non potuit, pedibus qui pontum per vada possent transire et magnos manibus divellere montis?'

vertere, 'to whirl' or 'dash,' transitive.

918. signi: partitive genit.

compacta, 'united into a single body.'

920. nunc quoque: definitely opposed to *tum*, l. 911.

921. laeta. l. 1372 'vineta laeta,' 'luxuriant.'

922. complexa : passive as in ii. 154 'complexa meant inter se'. See *complector, fin.*, Lewis and Short.

924. discrimina, 'their distinctive differences.'

926. quod=*quippe quod.*

928. fundatum, 'built on a firm foundation,' or, 'framework.' Wakefield compares Arnobius, 'ossibus illis fundata sunt corpora et nervorum colligatione devincta.' **viscera**, 'solid flesh,' as in l. 903.

929. Order 'nec quod facile caperetur': consecutive relative, 'not likely to be incapacitated': for this use of *capi* see Lewis and Short *capio* I. 1. e. ; cf. iv. 1022 'mentibu' capti'. Cic. *Tusc.* v. 40. 117 'oculis et auribus captus'.

ex aestu : i. e. by any results arising from heat.

930. labi : ablative as *igni*, ll. 1250, 1254.

931. volventia lustra : accus. of duration of time. *volventia* for *se volventia* ; see l. 831.

932. vulgivago : a Lucretian word : also in iv. 1071 with Venus.

933. moderator : also found with *equorum* or *arundinis* ; i. e. agriculture was still unknown, see note on l. 945. Wakefield compares Verg. *Aen.* viii. 316 'queis neque mos nec cultus erat'.

934. scibat : for *sciebat*, so ll. 949, 953 *scibant*, l. 1003 *saevibat*, l. 1324 *hauribant*. Duff adds *accibant*, l. 996. 'know how to'=ἐπίσταμαι with infinitive.

molirier. Cf. Verg. *Georg.* i. 494 'agricola incurvo terram molitus aratro'. Note the archaic infinit., a favourite usage with Lucretius ; cf. l. 979 *mirarier*, l. 1023 *miserarier*, l. 1199 *vertier*, l. 1250 *venarier*, ll. 1298, 1312 *moderarier*, l. 1379 *imitarier.*

935. defodere : l. 1366 'nova defodere in terram virgulta'= *inserere.*

936. falcibu' : here 'pruning-hooks,' a straighter and stronger instrument than the sickle. For omission of *s* see l. 824.

938. sponte sua. Cf. l. 872.

placabat, 'contented.' So in Hor. *Sat.* ii. 8. 5 'quae prima iratum ventrem placaverit esca'. Of quenching the thirst, Martial, i. 49 17 'avidam Dercenna placabit sitim'. We find a similar description of the rudeness of early life in Ov. *Met.* i. 103 'contentique cibis nullo cogente creatis arbuteos fetus montanaque fraga legebant cornaque . . . et mora . . . et glandes '.

donum = εὐεργέτημα, i. e. a boon bestowed by mother-earth and the sun.

939. glandiferas ... : Verg. *Georg.* i. 148 ' cum iam glandes atque arbuta sacrae deficerent silvae'.

941. arbuta : the fruit of the wild strawberry. Verg. *Georg.* ii. 519 'venit hiems : teritur Sicyonia baca trapetis, glande sues laeti redeunt, dant arbuta silvae'. Munro says that in December certain districts of the Peloponnese are bright with the scarlet fruit.

plurima etiam (=et) **maiora**, 'in great plenty and finer than nowadays.'

944. Though the food was coarse, yet there was abundance of it ; cf. Soph. *El.* 354 οὐ ζῶ ; κακῶς μέν, οἶδ᾽, ἐπαρκούντως δ᾽ ἐμοί.

945. sedare sitim ... vocabant : see passages quoted on l. 938. Ov. *Fast.* ii. 293 ' pro domibus frondes norant, pro frugibus herbas : nectar erat palmis hausta duabus aqua : nullus anhelabat sub adunco vomere taurus ; nulla sub imperio terra colentis erat '. Verg. *Aen.* viii. 316 ' queis neque mos nec cultus erat '. Notice the infin. after *vocare* instead of *ut.* Hor. *Od.* ii. 18. 38 ' hic levare functum pauperem laboribus vocatus '.

946. aquai : the archaic genitive of which Lucretius is so fond. l. 1099 *flammai*, l. 1124 *viai.*

947. claru' : of sound here and not of appearance : so appropriately with *citat* : cf. iv. 711 ' clara voce vocare '.

948. vagi : understand *nostri maiores.* The *silvestria templa* are well described by Verg. *Aen.* i. 166 ' fronte sub adversa scopulis pendentibus antrum, intus aquae dulces vivoque sedilia saxo, Nympharum domus '. For the asyndeton see ll. 1063-4.

949. scibant : see on *scibat* l. 934. Notice the inversion of **quibus e.** Observe the repetition of the letters *l, s*, and *u*, ' umori' fluenta lubrica proluvie larga lavere umida saxa, umida saxa, super viridi stillantia musco '. See note on l. 989.

lavere : the present infinitive for the more usual *lavare*, governed by *scibant.* Munro takes *lubrica* with *fluenta*, which is preferable to taking it with *saxa*, as *saxa* is not only separated from it by a number of words but also has its own epithet : again the second *umida saxa* loses force if it is merely a partial repetition of the whole phrase ' lubrica umida saxa '. For the repetition or ἐπανάληψις see l. 1402. In iii. 12 we find ' aurea dicta, aurea '.

951. stillantia : with *fluenta.*

952. scatere : here third conjugation, usually second : the infinit. depends on *scibant.* In l. 598 ' scatere atque erumpere lumen ', of the light of the sun.

953. igni tractare, ' to mould,' or ' prepare with fire ' : for **igni** cf. *labi* l. 930. We find an account of the discovery and benefits of fire in Aesch. *P. V.* 7 παντέχνου πυρὸς σέλας θνητοῖσιν ὤπασεν, and in 252 πῦρ ἐγώ σφιν ὤπασα ... ἀφ' οὗ γε πολλὰς ἐκμαθήσονται τέχνας. See the passages on fire l. 1011 and ll. 1091-1104 ; for **scibant** see l. 934.

954. spoliis : i. e. skins (Duff) : *exuviae* is often used in this sense. So we have *spolium leonis*, the skin of the Nemean lion : *spolium pecudis*, the golden fleece : *spolium viperei monstri*, Medusa's head. Cf. l. 1011.

955. We have a similar account of caves used as dwellings by primitive man in Aesch. *P. V.* 452 κατώρυχες δ' ἔναιον ... ἄντρων ἐν μυχοῖς ἀνηλίοις, and in Ovid. *Met.* i. 121 ' domus antra fuerunt et densi frutices et vinctae cortice virgae '. Munro says that *nemora* are cultivated woods or groves, while *silvae* are wild forests, but that the distinction is often lost sight of.

957. Notice the alliteration.

958. Neither the advantages nor the claims of society were recognized yet.

inter se : there was no idea of social life and obligation, and consequently no thought of right or law between man and man. Verg. *Aen.* viii. 316 ' queis neque mos nec cultus erat '.

scibant: as in l. 934.

960. **praedae**: either a partitive genitive depending on *quod* or possibly a predicative dative as in l. 875 ' praedae lucroque iacebant'.

cuique is masculine.

961. **sponte sua**, ' at his own discretion.'

quisque: note the emphatic force of *quisque* repeated after *cuique* : to be strong and to exert oneself solely for one's personal advantage was a characteristic of the early days among men as much as among beasts : see ll. 871-7, especially l. 875.

962. **in silvis** : as if they were mere beasts. Verg. *Aen.* iv. 165 ' speluncam Dido dux et Troianus eandem deveniunt : prima et Tellus et pronuba Iuno dant signum' ; also *Aen.* iv. 124.

963. **quamque**: sc. *mulierem*. Notice the alliteration in the next line.

965. **pretium** : the ἔδνα or dowry of the earliest bridegrooms is conceived as being a simple gift, but one that would strongly appeal to the simple desires of the age. Notice **atque** followed by **vel** : so in iii. 551 ' atque oculos naresve '.

966. Men had to rely on their natural forces in those days, and consequently these were highly developed as among the Red Indians, especially sight, hearing, smell, speed and strength.

968. **missilibus**, ' with stones for throwing.' Cf. Stat. *Theb.* viii. 524 ' uni sibi missile telum', a weapon which he alone can hurl.

magno pondere, upon which *clavae* depends, is ablative of description : cf. Caes. *B. G.* ii. 29 ' magni ponderis saxa', genitive of description.

969. **multa, pauca** : objects to the verbs.

vitabant pauca : in l. 985 ' spumigeri suis adventu validique leonis cedebant '.

970. **sūbus** : the dat. plur. is also *sŭbus* and *suibus*. Others read in this passage *sŭbŭ' sic*, ' just as they were,' without any elaborate preparations ; *sic = sicut erant*. Munro quotes Ov. *Fast.* vi. 331 ' Vesta iacet placidamque capit secura quietem, sicut erat, positum caespite fulta caput '.

971. **nuda dabant** : a brilliant restoration by Lambinus for MS. *nudabant*.

capti, ' overtaken ' or ' surprised,' at a distance from the cave which they had made their home.

972. **circum** is adverbial and does not govern *se* ; cf. note on *subter*, l. 1324. In order to escape being sighted or scented by wild beasts rather than to protect themselves from the cold. Similarly in the next line they avoid attracting the notice of animals by their cries, but rather endure in silence waiting for the break of day. Others suggest that the early races feared that the sun had actually died and would not return, an impossible view, for they had been accustomed to the setting and rising of the sun from their

earliest days, and would have been far more surprised if one day
the sun had never set at all.

977. **a parvis**=*a primis annis.*

979. Notice how Lucretius piles up his verbs to emphasize the
impossibility of the view. In vi. 727 he actually has 'fit uti fiat '.

mirarier: see *molirier* l. 934.

981. **detracto**: as if the disappearance of the sun had been caused
by some evil spirit or by enchantments. Cf. Verg. *Ecl.* viii. 69
'carmina vel caelo possunt deducere lunam'. Hor. *Epod.* v. 45
'Thessala lunam caelo deripit'.

982. **curae**: predicative dative.

983. **quietem**, 'repose.' There is no need to suppose that it is
either 'time of rest' or 'place of rest': the mere fact that their
vigilance was relaxed often proved fatal to them.

986. **intempesta nocte**, 'in the dead of night.' Verg. *Georg.* i.
247 'intempesta silet nox'; *Aen.* iii. 587 'nox intempesta'.
Conington compares νυκτὸς ἀωρί. On *intempestus* Varro says
'cum tempus agendi est nullum'.

cedebant, 'surrendered.'

987. The savage guests were the uninvited boar and lion.

988. **nimio plus**: usually 'too much,' here, 'much more,' a comparative use. In vi. 1196 'nec nimio post'. Plaut. *Bacch.* i. 2. 14
'quem ego sapere nimio censui plus quam Thalem'.

989. Notice the alliteration of the liquid *l.* Duff compares
Gray's *Elegy*, 'nor cast one longing lingering look behind.'

990. **unus quisque**, 'one or other.'

magis: sc. *quam nunc.*

991. **haustus**, 'rent '; cf. note on l. 1324 *hauribant*: so we have
in l. 1069 'suspensis teneros imitantur dentibus haustus'. See
Lewis and Short, *haurio*, I. B. 2.

992. i. e. the lairs where they had made their homes; cf. l. 955.

993. Notice the alliteration: the use of *v* (with a *w*-sound) was
felt to convey pathos. Verg. *Aen.* vi. 833 'neu patriae validas in
viscera vertite vires'. For **viscera** see on l. 903. Munro quotes
Spenser's *Faery Queene* ii. 8. 16 'but be entombed in the raven or
the kight.' Gorgias has γῦπες ἔμψυχοι τάφοι.

994. **adeso**, 'cruelly torn,' literally 'eaten into.'

995. **posterius**=ὕστερον, 'ever after.'

996. **accibant**: see on *scibat*, l. 934.

Orcum: god of the lower world and so the Lord and Giver of
Death.

997. **donec.** Lucretius has not used in any other passage the
construction of the pluperfect after *donec*, and Munro suggests that
possibly *privarunt* should be read or that perhaps the verb is
attracted into the pluperfect by the tense of *servarat.*

vermina. *Fest.* p. 375, Müll. 'vermina dicuntur dolores corporis
cum quodam minuto motu quasi a vermibus scindatur. Hic dolor
Graece στρόφος dicitur.' As στρόφος from στρέφω, so in Latin we
find *tormina* from *torqueo.* For the *v* alliteration see l. 993.

998. **vellent**, 'wanted ' or 'needed,' so as to be healed. Wake-

field mentions Bentley's citation of Sil. It. xi. 166 'medicinam vulnera poscunt'.

999. **at**: marking a strongly contrasted thought leading off from the preceding idea. Perhaps Lucretius is thinking of the bloodshed of the civil wars during his early life.

1000. In l. 95 we have 'una dies dabit exitio'. So in Enn. *Ann.* 8 '(milia) multa dies in bello conficit unus'.

1001. We have a picture of the reckless greed of merchants in Hor. *Od.* i. 1. 17 '(mercator) mox reficit rates quassas, indocilis pauperiem pati'.

lidebant, 'dashed'; the verb *lido* is found here only, but it is frequent in compounds *allido, collido, illido*.

1002. **hic**=*tum*.

temere incassum frustra, 'without aim, purpose, or result.' These three adverbs occur in ii. 1060 and are practically synonymous: see note on *multa modis multis*, l. 792.

1003. **saevibat**: see note on *scibat*, l. 934.

ponebat=*deponebat*.

inanis: to be taken predicatively.

1004. Notice the strong alliteration and also the repetition of *pellacia, pellicere* for the sake of emphasis. The sentiment is similar in ii. 559 'subdola cum ridet placidi pellacia ponti', but without any idea of treachery in i. 8 'tibi rident aequora ponti'.

1005. **in fraudem**, 'to his ruin.'

1006. 'When reckless seacraft was still a locked mystery to the ships,' as in the days before shipbuilding described in Ov. *Met.* i. 94 'nondum caesa suis peregrinum ut viseret orbem montibus in liquidas pinus descenderat undas, nullaque mortales praeter sua litora norant,' when men did not travel beyond their immediate neighbourhood.

1007. **tum deinde**, 'it was then too that . . .'

penuria=*inopia*, σπάνις.

1008. **mersat**: the object is *homines* understood. Munro seems to take *mersat* as if it were intransitive: 'sinks into ruin.' The meaning is that men dig their graves with their teeth, greater numbers dying from overeating than from want of food.

1009. Men used in their ignorance the juice of poisonous berries as a drink or possibly as a medicine. Duff quotes Verg. *Georg.* ii. 152 'nec miseros fallunt aconita legentes'.

1010. **vergebant**, 'poured out for themselves': so in Stat. *Theb.* vi. 211 'spumantesque mero paterae verguntur.' *vergere* means to tilt the vessel so as to pour out the contents.

nunc dant aliis: a correction for the MS. reading *nudant*. Munro suggested 'nurui nunc dant': 'now with nicer skill men give it to their son's wife instead,' i. e. to obtain her dowry. He quotes in support of his emendation Juv. xiv. 220 'elatam iam crede nurum, si limina vestra mortifera cum dote subit.' A passage might also be added from Ov. *Met.* i. 147 'lurida terribiles miscent aconita novercae'. Palmer proposed 'medici nunc dant . . . usi': 'now doctors prescribe and administer it,' with the meaning that though a large dose would be fatal, a doctor could use a poison in smaller quantities with good effects. But this is not so pointed and involves a further departure from the MSS.

1011. See the notes on ll. 953, 955.

pellis=*spolia ferarum* ; see l. 954.

1012. The beginnings of the formation of the family. Munro supplied the italicized line to complete the sense, which was defective owing to the loss of a verse.

lecti socialia iura, 'the ties and laws of wedlock.'

1015. **curavit ut**=*effecit ut.*

alsia, 'cold,' once in Lucretius, twice in Cicero: the word is connected with *algeo, alsi.*

ignis : see l. 953. Darwin says the discovery of fire was probably the greatest man ever made, excepting that of language.

1016. Contrast this with the hardier habits of l. 970-2, 'no longer as before.'

1017-8. Children began to take freer liberties with their parents.

1019. **amicitiem :** for *amicitiam.* l. 1047 *notities,* l. 1267 *materiem* ; iii. 59 *avarities.* This is the beginning of the social contract of mutual advantage between men.

1021. **commendarunt,** ' claimed indulgence for.'

muliebreque : see note on *esseque,* l. 874.

1022. **balbe :** with halting, stammering speech.

1023. **misererier :** see note on *molirier,* l. 934.

1024. **omnimodis.** Cf. 'multimodis (multi' modis), mirimodis (miri' modis)' : so this should be *omnibumodis.*

1025. **bona magnaque pars :** so in Ter. *Eun.* i. 2. 43 'bonam magnamque partem.' Duff compares ' pleno bene,' l. 708.

caste = *inviolata.*

1026. **aut** = εἰ δὲ μή, 'otherwise.'

1027. Cf. ll. 850, 856.

1028. There is a good description of the early life of mankind in Hor. *Sat.* i. 3. 99–111 :

> ' cum prorepserunt primis animalia terris,
> mutum et turpe pecus, glandem atque cubilia propter
> unguibus et pugnis, dein fustibus, atque ita porro
> pugnabant armis quae post fabricaverat usus,
> donec verba quibus voces sensusque notarent
> nominaque invenere : dehinc absistere bello,
> oppida coeperunt munire et ponere leges,
> ne quis fur esset, neu latro, neu quis adulter.
> . . . .
> iura inventa metu iniusti fateare necesse est.'

1029. **expressit** = *emittere coegit,* 'wrested,' 'elicited.' Lucretius holds the view that the names were given gradually by a natural instinct and desire on the part of the individual to express his wishes and feelings. Contrast with this view the account given in Genesis, where the story says that all animals were brought to Adam and he gave each one its name.

1030. 'In a very similar way inability to speak is in its turn seen to prompt infants to point and to beckon.'

infantia: Hor. *Sat.* ii. 5. 39 'seu rubra Canicula findet infantes statuas', 'statues that cannot speak.'

1032. **cum facit ut,** 'when it causes them to.'

sint: the subjunctive is possibly due to the feeling in Lucretius' mind that their reason for pointing is their wish to ask some question about the object: *sint* then is an indirect question.

1033. **vis**: for *viris* as in ii. 586, iii. 266.

vis: to be taken either (1) with *sentit*, 'as to his powers each man feels . . .'; this is probably the correct way of taking the passage, owing to the position of *quisque* between *vis* and *suas*, as it would be distinctly awkward to extract *quisque* from its enclosed place and to separate it from the two words that confine it : or (2) with *abuti*, which in Plaut. and Terence frequently governs the accusat. So we have in l. 358 'neque fungitur hilum'. Of *abutor* Duff says = ἀποχρῆσθαι here, often = καταχρῆσθαι.

quoad is scanned by synizesis as one long syllable ; cf. ll. 1213, 1433.

1034. **vitulo**: dative of possessor.

1035. **illis**: i.e. *cornibus.* Hor. *Od.* iii. 13. 3 'haedo, cui frons turgida cornibus primis et Venerem et proelia destinat '.

inurget: a rare word, 'pushes' or 'butts'. Hor. *Sat.* ii. 1. 52 'dente lupus, cornu taurus petit', and Verg. *Ecl.* iii. 87 '(taurus) cornu petat'. Wakefield adds Ov. *Hal.* 2 'vitulus sic nempe minatur qui nondum gerit in tenera iam cornua fronte ; sic dammae fugiunt, pugnant virtute leones, et morsu canis, et caudae sic scorpios ictu'. That is, in all animals we find that instinct causes them to act in the way natural to their kind, even before they have been taught by actual experience : this is worked out in the next few lines.

1036. **scymni**: a word characteristically chosen by Lucretius as being parallel to *catuli.*

iam tum, 'even at this early age.'

1040. **tremulum** well expresses the uncertain efforts of half-fledged birds in their earliest attempts at flight.

auxiliatum: ἅπ. λεγ. = *auxilium.* Cf. *summatum,* l. 1142.

1041. **proinde**: dissyllabic, 'and so.'

aliquem, 'one distinct person.'

inde refers back to the *aliquem,* 'and it was from him men learned' : cf. the use of *inde,* l. 1093.

putare is subject to *est.*

1045. Munro compares the same phrase in ll. 756, 765. In full it is equivalent to *tamen tempore eodem* : the phrase is to be taken with *putentur.*

non quisse (= *quivisse*): for *nequivisse.*

1047. **fuerant**: the pluperfect of the auxiliary marks a very strong pluperfect time.

notities: see note on *amicitiem,* l. 1019. This is a poetical, though not a strictly accurate translation of Epicurus' πρόληψις, which is preconception based on knowledge gained from former experiences; see the Introduction, 'Philosophy of Epicurus.' Cf. l. 182 'notities divis hominum unde est insita primum, quid vellent facere ut scirent animoque viderent?' i.e. what pattern for the creation of man could be present in the minds of the gods to enable them to realize what was their real object and wish? for if they had no preconceived idea of man, they could have no pattern to follow in their work of creation. So too if man had no preconception of voice he never either could or would have used it.

1048. huic: i.e. the *aliquem* of l. 1041.

1049. See note on 1047. Notice *scirēt* lengthened by the emphatic beat: so in English poetry, especially in the hymns we have frequent instances of syllables usually short being lengthened by the beat. The only other example in Lucretius is 'fulgēt' ii. 27.

but accentual in hymns! {handwritten margin note}

1050. cogere . . . victosque domare: see on l. 792.

1052. suadereque: see on *esseque*, l. 874. Successful efforts have recently been made, especially in America, to teach those who are both deaf and blind to talk.

1053. quid sit opus facto: *facto* depends on *opus*, which takes the ablative.

    quid is an accusat. of reference. See note on l. 844. In Terence *Ad.* iii. 4. 65 'moneo quid facto opus sit'. Plaut. *Truc.* v. 10 'opus est cibum'.

1054. amplius, 'further, longer, too long,' so 'continually.'

1057. vigeret: subjunctive after **cui** = *quippe cui*, Duff.

1058. pro vario sensu, 'according to their different emotions,' pleasure, grief or fear, &c.; cf. l. 1061 and note on l. 1063.

1059. mutae: of inarticulate sounds, see note on l. 1088.

    denique, 'actually.'

1061. gliscunt: literally 'swell,' i.e. their hearts swell with joy or passion (**dolor**, 'resentment'); cf. iv. 1069 'inque dies gliscit furor'.

1062. quippe etenim: so in l. 1169 a redundant expression = 'for.'

    rebus apertis, 'from plain' or 'obvious facts.' So in iv. 467. 'nam nil aegrius est quam res secernere apertas ab dubiis'.

1063. Munro quotes Darwin: 'the dog since being domesticated has learnt to bark in at least four or five distinct tones.' Molossi (*canes* is often omitted) were a famous breed of large dogs celebrated throughout all Latin literature.

1064. mollia ricta, 'spongy open lips.'

    ricta: an irregular plural from collateral form *rictum* as in vi. 1195. Observe the number of adjectives without connecting particles; asyndeton is very common in Lucretius; cf. ll. 948, 1096, 1436.

1065. restricta: bare or show their teeth, as in Quint. *Decl.* xii. 27 'restrictis labris'.

1066. et cum, 'than when . . .' so again in ll. 1067, 1071, 1077. After *alius*, *ac* or *atque* is more common than *et*; see note on l. 1260.

    iam, 'outright.'

omnia : sc. *loca.*

1069. 'pretend to bite them gently with lightly closing jaws.' Munro seems to put it rather too strongly : ' a feint of swallowing them.' For **haustus** see note on l. 991. Munro quotes a passage, ' nec blandis mihi morsibus renides,' from an epigram on a pet dog, Myia, written perhaps in the first century A. D., and found at Agen à Auch in South France : apparently it is in imitation of Catull. iii.

1070. **alio pacto**=*alia ratione*; cf. l. 1281; it is common through-out Latin.

gannitu, ' yelping.'

adulant : rarer than *adulantur*, ' caress,' literally, ' fawn on.'

1071. **et cum** : as above, l. 1066.

baubantur, ' bay,' ἀπ. λεγ.

1072. **plorantes,** ' whining ' or ' howling.'

summisso corpore, ' crouching,' with the tail between the legs.

1074. **iuvencus** : the adjective is rare in this use : the word is more common as a substantive or with *bos* understood. It is also used of young men and maidens.

1075. **pinnigeri.** Cf. l. 737 'Veneris praenuntius ante pennatus graditur '.

calcaribus amoris: so we have in Verg. *Georg.* iii. 209 ' sed non ulla magis vires industria firmat quam Venerem et caeci stimulos avertere amoris, sive boum sive est cui gratior usus equorum '.

1076. ' he snorts out the alarm ' : **ad arma,** *aux armes,* this is the cry of the sentinel warning his comrades, here of the horse snorting to attract his mate.

1077. **sic alias**=at any chance time.

concussis artubus : his limbs pulsing and quivering with life.

1078. Notice the redundancy of expression.

1079. **ossifragae,** ' osprey,' which is itself derived from the Latin. Again the phraseology is tautological, *marinis fluctibus in salso victum vitamque,* as in l. 1105. *salsum* is here a noun. Duff compares *in tranquillo,* used as a substantive, l. 12.

1081. **iaciunt**=*mittere*, l. 1029. Duff's theory that some line, as ' et cum progeniem parvam nidosque revisunt ', cf. Verg. *Georg.* i. 414 ' iuvat progeniem parvam dulcesque revisere nidos,' has dropped out, is not only improbable owing to the double **et cum** in different senses so close together, but also absolutely unnecessary, for Lucretius says birds frequently utter cries quite distinct from those that they make when fighting over their prey : there is no need to add another point of difference.

1082. **praedaeque . . .,** ' struggle with their prey ' : if *praeda* is read, it is governed by *de.*

1083. **tempestatibus,** ' along with the changes of weather.' Take *una* with *cum* : for the inversion cf. l. 1228.

1084. **cornicum ut saecla vetusta** : crows, rooks, and ravens are said to be long-lived.

1085. This superstitition is mentioned in Verg. *Georg.* i. 388 ' cornix plena pluviam vocat improba voce '. Notice the redundancy of expression in l. 1086.

1087. Cf. l. 1061.

muta : of inarticulate sounds, so in l. 1059.

1089. tum : emphatic.

aequum, 'natural,' right and fair by the rules of natural supe-riority.

1091. For this and the following lines which amplify Lucretius' former remarks about fire, cf. l. 953 and note.

ne forte requiras : final not imperative ; cf. ' ne forte credas ', l. 890.

1093. primitus : ante- and post-classical.

inde, ' and from it,' as in l. 1042.

1095. fulgĕre. Cf. vi. 165 in the same position in the line.

plaga ' the bolt of heaven has filled them with its glowing heat ; ' cf. l. 1220.

1096. et tamen, ' and apart from that,' as in l. 1177, i. e. the following reason is in itself a sufficiently strong argument. Notice the two unconnected participles in addition to an adjective ; see note on l. 1064. Cf. with this passage i. 897–900 ' fit . . . ut altis arboribus vicina cacumina summa terantur inter se, validis facere id cogentibus austris, donec flammai fulserunt flore coorto.'

1097. aestuat, ' sways about,' others translate, ' grows hot.' But cf. ' fretis aestuosis ', Hor. Od. ii. 7. 16. aestus is used in the same sense of turmoil and violent motion, l. 1435 ' belli magnos commovit aestus'.

1099. flammai : see on aquai, l. 946.

1100. mutua : adverbial neuter plural, as in iv. 301, for mutuo, which is impossible in hexameters.

1101. utrumque : subject to potest, ' either of these causes.'

1104. verberibus : a strong word of the heat caused by the striking of the sun's rays ; cf. plaga, πληγή. In l. 484 we have ' radii solis cogebant terram verberibus crebris in artum.'

1105. victum vitamque. Cf. note on l. 1079. The poetry from ll. 1105–1240 includes some of the finest in this book.

1106. rebu' : ablative of exchange.

1108. The beginnings of a more united and elaborate civilization : see the quotation from Horace on l. 1028.

1109. Duff recalls the original meaning of praesidium (from praesidere, a place to rule in). It is, however, more in accordance with Lucretius' custom to redouble his synonyms for emphasis rather than to search for slight differences in meaning, which had practically vanished in his time.

1111. The personal qualities of men, from which owing to a strongly hereditary tendency an aristocracy was gradually evolved. Monarchy is the earliest form of government after the first com-bination of families : this is followed by a monarchy tempered by an aristocratic element. Later comes the time when power of wealth supersedes influence of rank and gradually a plutocracy or democracy becomes the final governing principle.

1112. vigebant, ' were held in high honour.'

1113. res, ' property,' ' wealth.' Lucretius deplores the power of wealth as Ovid in *Met.* i. 140 'effodiuntur opes, irritamenta malorum: iamque nocens ferrum ferroque nocentius aurum prodierat', and as Horace in *Od.* iii. 3. 49 'aurum irrepertum et sic melius situm cum terra celat'. Cf. l. 1241 and following.

1115. Lambinus quotes Hor. *Sat.* ii. 3. 94 'omnis enim res, virtus, fama, decus, divina humanaque pulchris divitiis parent', and following.

sectam sequuntur, 'follow in the train of.' Catull. lxiii. 15 'Gallae sectam meam exsecutae, duce me, mihi comites'; Cic. *N. D.* ii. 22. 57 'omnis natura habet quasi viam quandam et sectam quam sequatur'.

1116. **creti** : see note on *concreta*, l. 798.

1117-35. It has been suggested that these lines on the evils of ambition were written with reference to incidents in Memmius' life.

1118. **vivere parce** : the subject to *sunt*; notice the verb is attracted into the plural by the plural predicate *divitiae*. Wakefield quotes Hes. *Op.* 40 νήπιοι, οὐδὲ ἴσασιν ὅσῳ πλέον ἥμισυ παντός, i. e. enough is as good as a feast.

1119. 'There is never lack of little.'

1120. **claros voluerunt se.** Munro quotes Plaut. *Trin.* iii. 2. 38 'cum te maxume clarum voles'.

1123. **succedere** depends on *certantes*. Gray's *Elegy* 'the paths of glory lead but to the grave'. We have 'in summum successit honorem', l. 1275.

1124. **iter viai** : so in ii. 626 'iter viarum'. For **viai** cf. l. 946.

1126. **invidia** : either the envy of unsuccessful rivals (*certantes*, l. 1124) or more probably, as Duff suggests, 'this *invidia* bears some resemblance to the Nemesis or envy of the gods in the old mythology, which Lucretius utterly discards'. In the same way in ll. 1136-40 Nemesis falls on kings, and in ll. 1231-2 on fleets. For the same reason, when a man was uncertain whether to marry a rich lady above him in rank or a poor one of his own position, Pittacus, the sage, advised him to choose the latter, telling him to watch children spinning their tops in the street and saying each to his own top τὴν κατὰ σαυτὸν ἔλαυνε, 'keep in your own line'. Cf. Arist. Clouds 25 ἔλαυνε τὸν σαυτοῦ δρόμον.

contemptim almost = *contemptos* predicative. Notice the *t* alliteration.

1127. **vaporant:** *vaporo* is found here only used intransitively in sense of 'burn', 'are blasted by the breath of envy.' Aeschylus gives a vivid description of Nemesis in *P. V.* 360 ὃς (Ζεὺς) αὐτὸν ἐξέπληξε τῶν ὑψηγόρων κομπασμάτων. ἐφεψαλώθη κἀξεβροντήθη σθένος ... κεραυνῷ Ζηνὸς ἠνθρακωμένος, where the thunderbolt of Zeus fell on and blasted the boastful offender.

1128. **et quae . . .,** 'and all that is raised aloft above the level of other things.'

quae . . . cumque : in tmesis; see on l. 883.

aliis : ablative of comparison, probably neuter as *summa*.

1130. Vergil holds a different opinion in *Aen.* vi. 851 'tu regere imperio populos, Romane, memento'.

1131. proinde: dissyllabic as in l. 1041.

sine: addressing each reader individually.

sanguine sudent: see Lewis and Short, *sudo*, I. A. β; Luke xxii. 44; Hesiod, *Op.* 289 τῆς δ᾽ ἀρετῆς ἱδρῶτα θεοὶ προπάροιθεν ἔθηκαν ἀθάνατοι· μακρὸς δὲ καὶ ὄρθιος οἶμος ἐς αὐτὴν καὶ τρηχύς. Duff quotes the French proverb 'suer sang et eau', to exert oneself excessively.

1133. Men are too ready to follow the majority and go with the stream of public opinion: also they do not trouble to think for themselves, and so the faculties gradually become weaker and more rudimentary from disuse. Duff adds Hor. *Ep.* i. 16. 19 'vereor ne cui de te plus quam tibi credas'.

1135. 'And this is no more good at the present time nor will it be in the future . . .'

1136. The Nemesis and *invidia* of l. 1126 fell on the kings of old times. Notice participle and adjective to *maiestas*.

1137. soliorum: an unusual plural attracted probably by the number of *sceptra*, which in the abstract sense is generally used in the plural; see on l. 1234.

1138. 'The glorious badge of the sovereign head,' i. e. the crown. **insigne** is a substantive.

cruentum must be taken with **sub pedibus lugebat**.

1140. conculcatur. Cf. ll. 1234–5.

metutum: the only instance of the passive of *metuo*, with the exception of *metuendus*. Juvenal gives a lurid picture of the malevolence of the mob in *Sat.* x. 66 'Seianus ducitur unco spectandus: gaudent omnes. "quae labra, quis illi vultus erat. numquam amavi hunc hominem"'.

1141. res: either (1) 'things came at length into complete ruin and confusion', **ad summam faecem turbasque**, 'to the lees of the utmost disorder,' or (2) = *summa res*, 'the sovereign power passed into the hands of the lowest of the mob' where *ad summam faecem turbasque* means 'to the mere dregs of the people and to mob-rule.'

redibat is probably emphatic, returned, went back to the disorder of the earliest times previous to the government of kings.

1142. summatum, ἅπ. λεγ.=*summum imperium*. Cf. *auxiliatum*, l. 1040.

1143. From **partim** we get the subject to *docuere*, as in l. 1310. Compare the development of the power of the plebs in the early history of Rome.

1144. constituere is of course the perfect.

1145. defessum: common with infinitive in Plautus, as *lassus* with the same construction in Propertius.

1149. aequis: emphatic, legal t. t. 'equity,' or case-law, where the circumstances of the case are taken into consideration.

1150. pertaesum: more common with the genitive than with the infinitive.

1151. inde: from the punishment that is now meted out to those avengers who take the law into their own hands.

1152. i.e. all who commit violence and wrong are likely to find their evil deeds recoil on their own heads.

1153. Wakefield quotes Hes. *Op.* 265 οἷ αὐτῷ κακὰ τεύχει ἀνὴρ ἄλλῳ κακὰ τεύχων, ἡ δὲ κακὴ βουλὴ τῷ βουλεύσαντι κακίστη, i.e. they fall into pits that they have dug for others : they are hoist with their own petard.

1156. This is not an inconsistency in Lucretius, who held the view that the gods entirely disregarded the affairs of mortals : he means that if a man does believe, whether rightly or wrongly, in the existence of the gods he ought to act on his belief and dread divine retribution on his misdeeds.

1157. Cf. Psalms xiv. 1 and liii. 1, ' The fool hath said in his heart, There is no God.' 'But,' says Bacon, 'he does not believe it '; he says it merely to encourage himself.

clam : an adverb instead of an adjective, which would be more usual with *fore.* Munro : 'he cannot but feel a misgiving that his secret (id) can be kept for ever'. So also in Cic. *de Fin.* i. 16. 50 'quamvis occulte fecerit, numquam tamen id confidet fore semper occultum '.

1158. se : to be taken with protraxe = *protraxisse,* 'have given themselves away.'

protraxe in medium : as in l. 1454 'protrahit in medium '. Compare iv. 1011-14, where Lucretius says that men during their sleep and in their dreams carry out their most deeply cherished wishes and plans.

1161. numina pervulgarit, 'spread abroad the worship of . . .' Lucretius will now set forth the beginnings of religion.

1163. sollemnia, 'recurring at stated intervals.' Notice *sācra* followed by *săcra*; cf. l. 839 'interŭtrasque nec ūtrum ūtrimque'; so in iv. 1222 'quae pătribus pātres '; iv. 1259 'lĭquidis et lĭquida '; so Homer has Ἄρɛς Ἄρɛς.

1164. This sentence is an adjectival clause.

rebu', 'occasions.'

1166. suscitat = *aedificat,* 'raises,' i.e. makes men raise.

1167. celebrare, 'to throng them'; so i. 4 'terras concelebras'.

1168. non ita difficilest : exactly the English idiom, ' it is not so hard': on this line depends the construction of the indirect questions, ll. 1161-3.

1169. quippe etenim : see note on l. 1062.

1170. Waking visions or trances, ὕπαρ, opposed to l. 1171, dreams in sleep, ὄναρ. Duff remarks that in ll. 148-9, 'tenvis enim natura deum longeque remota sensibus ab nostris animi vix mente videtur,' Lucretius seems to be inconsistent. But Lucretius means that so fine is the nature of the matter of which the gods are composed that the senses of man (sight, hearing) are quite unable to perceive it, and only the mind, i.e. that part of man which is composed of the finest atoms, is able to receive any impression of it.

1171. mirando auctu : ablative of quality.

et magis, 'and still more.'

1172. **tribuebant,** 'attributed'; cf. *tribuit,* l. 1195: so *tradere,* l. 1187, *dabant,* l. 1175, and *relinquunt,* l. 1239.

1174. **pro,** 'to match.'

1176. **suppeditabatur,** 'was brought up before them,' 'rose up before their eyes.'

manebat, 'appeared unchanged'; cf. l. 830 'manet sui similis res'. Therefore men imagined that these divinities were immutable and immortal.

1177. **et tamen:** see note on l. 1096; with **omnino,** 'and yet without all this.' With **auctos** understand *deos.*

1178. **temere,** 'lightly' or 'easily'.

convinci. Munro says Lucretius often uses *vinco* for *convinco*: to this use of *convinci* for *vinci* there is no parallel case. Duff quotes Shakespeare, *Macbeth,* i. 7. 64, 'his two chamberlains Will I with wine and wassail so convince,' i.e. overcome.

1179. **fortunis:** they believed that the happiness of the gods far exceeded their own.

1180. **vexaret:** subjunctive, as expressing their thought, not necessarily the true reason, a semi-sneer on the part of Lucretius at the credulity of these god-worshippers.

1182. **inde:** i.e. 'ab operibus suis'.

1183. **caeli rationes,** 'the system of the heavens,' i.e. the series or cycle of natural phenomena, e.g. *tempora,* 'the seasons,' the waning and waxing of the moon, &c.

1185. Compare Vergil's line that refers to Lucretius, *Georg.* ii. 490 'felix qui potuit rerum cognoscere causas'.

1186. 'And so they considered it to be their last resource to attribute everything to the gods and to make everything subject to their will.'

perfugium, a complementary accusative to tradere et facere, infinitives to be treated as nouns.

1188. **templa:** here used in the older sense of 'realms' or 'quarters of the sky', as it is in ll. 1205, 1436, and in i. 1014 'caeli lucida templa'. Epicurus maintained that the gods lived not in the sky but in the spaces between the worlds, μετακόσμια.

1189. **sol:** a reading suggested for MS. *nox* which occurs again in the next line.

1190. The substantives in this line and the next are subjects to *volvi videtur.* Notice the repetition of *luna.*

signa severa, 'the still, cold stars,' 'the austere stars': l. 1210 'candida sidera'.

1191. **faces,** 'meteors': ii. 206 'nocturnasque faces'. Vergil describes them well in *Georg.* i. 367 '(videbis) flammarum longos a tergo albescere tractus'. Notice the repetition **flammaeque volantes,** 'fiery comets.'

1192. A remarkable case of asyndeton; cf. ll. 1372, 1448-9.

1193. Notice the force given by the *m* alliteration as the culmination of the catalogue of phenomena, 'the terrors of the threatening thunderbolt'; cf. l. 1221.

1194. **genus** : probably the exclamatory accusative. Duff compares ii. 14 'o miseras hominum mentes ! '

1195. **tribuit** : as in l. 1172.

iras : men in their folly assigned human passions to the gods, though, as Munro says, '"neque tangitur irā" was an essential of the divine nature according to Epicurus and Lucretius'. So Verg. *Aen.* i. 11 'tantaene animis caelestibus irae?'

1198. **pietas**, 'no act of piety is it to be often seen.'

velatum : the Romans prayed *velato capite,* the Greeks *aperto capite.*

1199. **vertier** : see note on l. 934. Munro : 'the suppliant approached in such a way as to have the statue of the god on his right and then after praying wheeled to the right so as to front it, and then prostrated himself : προσκυνεῖν περιφερομένους.'

ad lapidem : either (1) contemptuously on the part of Lucretius, 'a mere stone,' 'the work of men's hands,' or possibly a diorite or meteoric stone, or (2) one of the busts of Janus or perhaps one of the *termini* (boundary stones) which were held sacred by the Romans.

1200. Notice the strong *p* alliteration.

pandere palmas : i.e. with the palms uppermost as in Verg. *Aen.* iv. 205 'multa Iovem manibus supplex orasse supinis ', and in Aesch. *P. V.* 1005 λιπαρεῖν ὑπτιάσμασιν χερῶν.

1202. **votis nectere vota** : either (1) to reel off one prayer after another as a selfish man might do, making no end to his wishes as in Pers. *Sat.* v. 53 'nec voto vivitur uno ', or (2) as the rows of votive tablets which were hung up on the walls of the temples in return for blessings already vouchsafed and setting forth petitions still to be granted, *votivae tabulae.*

1203. **sed mage**, 'but rather,' an apocop. form of *magis*, being originally *magi*', then *magi*, finally changing to *mage* as *pote* of *potis* in iii. 1079. An untroubled conscience is the possession of the really good man.

1205. **templa** : as in ll. 1188, 1436.

fixum : for the fixity of the sky we may compare l. 511 'ex utraque polum parti premere aera nobis dicendum est extraque tenere et claudere utrimque ', and for its revolution i. 2 'caeli subter labentia signa ', and Ov. *Met.* ii. 204 'altoque sub aethere fixis incursant stellis ' ; the two ideas should be combined, i.e. the revolution of the sky on a fixed axis.

1206. Notice this impersonal construction with a genitive probably on the analogy of the genitive after verbs such as *reminiscor* : this construction is common in Cicero, see Lewis and Short, *mens,* II. B. The more usual construction is the personal subject.

1207. **oppressa** : to be taken with *pectora.*

1208. **expergefactum caput erigere** : i.e. 'se expergefacere et consurgere atque intrare pectora nostra '.

1209. **nobis** : ethic dative, 'we may find to our cost' ; cf. l. 805.

immensa : in its primary sense, 'boundless.' This is one of the lines which seem to shadow certain misgivings in the mind of Lucretius about the power of the gods ; cf. ll. 1156-7.

1211. 'Inability to solve the riddle of the universe distracts man's mind.'

dubiam is predicative.

1213. finis: feminine, as in l. 826.

quoad: monosyllabic as in ll. 1033, 1433=*quatenus*.

1214. laborem, 'the strain of restless motion,' pulling now in one direction, now in another; cf. l. 1272 'durum sufferre laborem'.

1215. donata: to be taken with *moenia*. Munro: 'or gifted by the grace of the gods with an everlasting existence they may glide on through a never-ending tract of time and defy the strong powers of immeasurable ages'; a fine translation of a fine piece of poetry. l. 1216 recurs in i. 1004, l. 1217 in l. 379 of this book.

1219. animus contrahitur: we find a similar expression in Cic. *Lael.* xiii. 48 'ut et bonis amici quasi diffundantur (expand) et incommodis contrahantur'. For **correpunt membra** cf. l. 1223 'corripiunt membra'.

1220. plaga: see note on l. 1095. For **murmura** cf. l. 1193 'murmura magna minarum'.

1223. corripiunt governs **membra**; in l. 1219 *membra* is subject to *correpunt*.

1224. nequid ob admissum: for *ne ob quid admissum*.

1225. poenarum solvendi: either (1) a combination of (*a*) gerund, *poenas solvendi*, (*b*) gerundive, *poenarum solvendarum*, the object being to avoid harsh and cumbrous terminations (see Roby, *Lat. Gram.* Pt. ii. p. lxviii), or better (2) *poenarum* depends on *solvendi*, which is to be taken as a substantive, both being objective genitives, 'the time of the paying of the penalty.'

adultum: Lachmann's suggestion for *adauctum*; cf. l. 800.

1227. induperatorem: see on l. 876.

cum ... pariter=*una cum*; for the inversion of the usual order see note, l. 1083.

1229. divum pacem, 'the grace and favour of heaven,' in this case manifested by *ventorum paces*, 'a lull in the storm.' Notice **adit**=*implorare*. Munro quotes the same use of *adire* in Apul. *Met.* vi. 3 'adire cuiuscumque dei veniam'.

animas=*auras* as in vi. 693 'ne dubites quin haec animai turbida sit vis', and in Hor. *Od.* iv. 12. 2 'impellunt animae lintea Thraciae.'

1231. saepe, 'in many an instance'=*ut saepe fit*.

1232. nilo ... minus: for *nihilominus*.

ad vada leti=*ad letalia vada*.

1233. vis abdita: the secret power and inscrutable working of nature.

1234. obterit: so *proculcare* next line and *conculcatur*, l. 1140.

fascis saevasque securis: the phrase is repeated in iii. 996 'petere a populo fascis saevasque securis'. In l. 1137 the insignia of the highest offices ('sceptra superba et praeclarum insigne') are used for the power they confer, 'greatness.'

ludibrio: predicative dative; cf. *vitio vertere*, l. 1357.

1236. vacillat: as the result of an earthquake; so in vi. 575 'vacillant omnia tecta'.

1237. dubiaeque minantur, 'threaten to fall.' Duff compares Sen. *N. D.* vi. 1. 2 'oppidi pars ruit dubieque stant etiam quae relicta sint'.

1239. relinquunt=*tribuebant*, l. 1172, 'assign.'

1240. in rebus : i. e. in things on earth.

quae is consecutive.

1241. quod superest=τοιαῦτα μὲν δὴ ταῦτα, so much for that, 'to continue'; it marks a transition. Cf. note on l. 1113.

1242. argenti pondus, plumbi potestas. Lucretius is very fond of periphrasis, and instead of naming the material or substance alone he prefers to add to it its especial properties or qualities ; cf. l. 1286 'ferri vis aerisque', l. 1281 'ferri natura '.

potestas, 'the potentiality' or 'useful qualities '.

1245. bellum silvestre : the mode of warfare natural to savage tribes and primitive man.

1246. formidinis ergo: 'to inspire terror ' : **ergo,** 'for the sake of,' is found in Cato, Livy, Cicero, and Vergil, yet it was held by those who used it to be an archaic preposition.

1248. pandere, ' to clear ' or ' open up ' = ψιλοῦν. Duff also compares ψιλὴ γῆ, 'arable land.'

pascua : adjective and predicative, ' fit for pasture.'

1250. fovea, 'pitfall'; so in Hor. *Ep.* i. 16. 50 ' cautus enim metuit foveam lupus '.

igni : ablative, as in l. 1254 ; see l. 930.

venarier : a substantival infinitive ; for the form see note on l. 934.

1252. quidquid id est, ' whatever the cause may be.'

1254. percoxerat : the heat penetrated into the very vitals of the earth.

igni : as in l. 1250.

1255. See note on l. 911. **venis ferventibus,** ' from the glowing veins.'

1257. concreta : i. e. cooled and moulded into lumps ; cf. l. 798.

videbant=the optative of indefinite frequency, a Graecism frequently imitated by Livy.

1259. lēvi, 'smooth and polished.'

1260. ' Moulded into shapes similar to the outlines of the cavities in which each lump lay.'

simili atque : see note on l. 1066.

1262. penetrabat eos, ' it gradually occurred to them ' : the word implies that it took some time for the idea to penetrate. Wakefield quotes Tac. *Ann.* iii. 4 'nihil tamen Tiberium magis penetravit quam studia hominum accensa in Agrippinam', but this is not parallel use, for here *penetravit*=*vexavit*. For the use of the impersonal verb see the note on l. 795.

1264. Munro : ' and could by hammering out be brought to tapering points of any degree of sharpness and fineness '.

prorsum, 'absolutely,' ' perfectly,' is less commonly used than the form *prorsus*.

quamvis, ' as far as one could wish.'

· **1266. tela**=ὅπλα, 'instruments' or 'tools' for agriculture, &c. : the use of metals for weapons was a later development; cf. the next paragraph. The subject to **parent** is *haec metalla* understood, to **possent**, *ipsi* understood.

1267. materiemque dolare, 'hew timber and plane smooth the planks.'

lēvia: predicatively. For the form **materiem** see note on l. 1019.

1268. perque forare: tmesis; see note on l. 883 : *terebrare*, to bore a hole with a gimlet ; *perforare*, to pierce with a bradawl; *pertundere*, to punch a hole.

1270. violentis viribus, 'with masterful might.'

1272. laborem, 'strain,' as in l. 1214.

pariter: i. e. *cum aere*. In l. 1359 we have again 'pariter durum sufferre laborem '.

1273. iacebat, 'lay neglected.'

1274. hebeti mucrone: oxymoron, ablative of description.

1275. Cf. l. 1123 ' ad summum succedere honorem '.

1276. volvenda aetas, 'time as it rolls on'; so in l. 931 ' volventia lustra '. In Lucretius the gerundive is the equivalent of the present participle in meaning ; so too we find in Verg. *Aen.* ix. 7 ' volvenda dies '=*dies se volvens*.

1277. nullo honore: ablative of description. For the sentiment of ll. 1276-8 cf. ll. 831-3. l. 1278 is practically a repetition of l. 833.

1279. appetitur, 'is coveted.'

laudibus: ablative of attendant circumstances. For **in dies** cf. ll. 1307, 1370 of daily increase, opposite to *quotidie* which implies no increase.

1281. quo pacto = *quomodo* ; cf. l. 1070.

ferri natura: a periphrasis for *ferrum* ; cf. l. 1286 ' ferri vis aerisque ', and the note on l. 1242.

1283. Horace gives a similar description in *Sat.* i. 3. 101 ' unguibus et pugnis, dein fustibus, atque ita porro pugnabant armis quae post fabricaverat usus '.

1285. cognita: neuter plural agreeing with feminine and masculine subjects which are impersonal.

1286. ferri vis: see note on l. 1242.

1288. quo: Duff= ὅσῳ, 'because' ; often used when the sentence contains a comparative.

facilis, 'ductible,' 'easy to work.'

natura is nominative.

1289. tractabant, 'till': so in *Col.* ii. 4. 5 'lutosum agrum tractari '. Hesiod describes the tools of primitive agriculture *Op.* 151 χαλκῷ δ' εἰργάζοντο· μέλας δ' οὐκ ἔσκε σίδηρος.

aereque: see note on *esseque*, l. 874. For **belli fluctus** cf. l. 1435 ' belli aestus '.

1290. serebant: surely from *serere*, 'to sow'; cf. Lucan, who uses the same metaphor in viii. 352 ' vulnera nostra in Scythicos spargis populos '. Munro suggests that it possibly comes from *serere*, 'to plait.'

56

1291. ollis : archaic form of *illis*, so in l. 1390, not uncommon in Vergil. The construction is *dativus commodi*.

1292. inerma : a rare form, found in Cic. *Fam.* xi. 12. 1 ' cum paucis inermis ' and also in Sallust. Lucretius has also ii. 845 *sterila* for *sterilia*, i. 340 ' *sublima* for *sublimia*, ii. 1122 *hilaro* for *hilari*.

1294. species, ' the very appearance of a copper sickle,' or possibly only a Lucretian periphrasis for *falx*. Duff renders it, though not so forcibly, ' the fashion.' In Vergil the sickle becomes the sword, *Georg.* i. 508 ' et curvae rigidum falces conflantur in ensem '. For **versaque in opprobrium**, v. l. *obscenum*, ' fell into disgrace,' cf. l. 1357 ' vitio vertere '.

1295. This line amplifies l. 1286.

1296. exaequata : as the Romans found the iron sword of their legionaries gave them a great advantage over the copper sword of the German tribes, which bent at every blow. But when all men used iron swords then the fights were contested on equal terms.

creperi, ' wavering ' ; originally dusky, obscure, hence uncertain = *ancipitis Martis*.

1297. prius est, ' it is an earlier custom ; cf. *ante fuit*, l. 1380.

conscendere is a substantive and is subject to *est*.

1298. moderarier : for the form see note on l. 934. Here *moderarier* governs the accusative, in l. 1312 it takes the dative.

dextraque vigere, ' to show prowess with the right hand,' while the left holds the bridle.

1300. We have the same construction in this line as in l. 1297.

1301. falciferos : Livy uses the word *falcatus*. The Britons, Gauls, and Germans employed these scythe-wheeled chariots.

1302. boves lucas : so called because the Romans first saw elephants in Lucania in the army of King Pyrrhus, as the story is told in Plin. *N. H.* viii. 6. 16.

turrito : so in Sil. Ital. iv. 601 ' vis elephantorum turrito concita dorso ' ; cf. the quotation from Livy on l. 1315.

1303. anguimanus : as in ii. 537 ' anguimanus elephantos ' ; Ov. *Met.* i. 184 ' anguipedum.'

1305. alid : for *aliud*, as in ll. 257, 1456.

1306. quod is final relative.

1307. in dies : see note on l. 1279.

augmen : a favourite word with Lucretius, in other writers it is rare.

1308. in moenere belli, ' in the service of war.' Hannibal used oxen with another object, when he fastened lighted faggots on their horns to mislead the Romans.

1310. partim = *nonnulli* ; see the note on l. 1143 for the construction.

1311. No distinction between **doctoribus** and **magistris** is intended.

1312. qui is final relative.

moderarier : with dative, contrast l. 1298. For the form see note on l. 934.

LUCRETIUS V. 1314-31

1314. turbabant : the subject is *leones* understood from l. 1310.

1315. These were not the manes and crests of the wild beasts, but were artificial and were intended partly to protect the head but chiefly to inspire terror, as in Liv. xxxvii. 40. 4 'ingentes ipsi (elephanti) erant : addebant speciem frontalia et cristae et tergo impositae turres'. In Vergil we have the natural crest of the lion mentioned, *Aen*. xii. 6 'tum demum movet arma leo, gaudetque comantes excutiens cervice toros'.

1316. fremitu : sc. *leonum*.

1318. irritata : transference of epithet which properly belongs to *leae*.

leae is poetical for *leaenae*.

1319. adversum . . ., 'would strike in the face these who met them.' **adversum** is an adverb and is to be taken with **venientibus**, which is dative of the possessor. Duff compares 'on lui trancha la tête'.

1320. nec opinantis : accusative agreeing with the unexpressed object of *deripiebant,* 'would tear down.'

1321. deplexae, ἄπ. λεγ. from *deplector,* 'twining round them.'

dabant in terram, 'dragged them to the ground'; Liv. xxxi. 37. 9 'rex, ruente saucio equo, praeceps ad terram datus'.

adfixae = *inhaerentes,* 'fastening on them.'

1324. hauribant : for the form see note on *scibat,* l. 934, for the meaning see on *haustus,* l. 991. Livy uses the same expression in a similar context vii. 10. 10 'uno alteroque ictu ventrem atque inguina hausit '.

subter : an adverb, as in l. 1364, and compare *infra,* l. 1371, and *circum,* ll. 972, 1378, 1437.

1325. terram ruebant, 'scored' or 'ploughed up the earth', as in vi. 726 'cum mare permotum ventis ruit intus harenam'. There is a similar idea in Verg. *Ecl*. iii. 86 'pascite taurum, iam cornu petat et pedibus qui spargat harenam '.

fronte : i. e. *cornu.*

1327. This line is followed in the MSS. by a verse **in se fracta suo tinguentes sanguine tela,** which is probably spurious, and was written as a gloss to explain the word **infracta** as equivalent to *in se fracta,* 'broken off short in their bodies,' for there is also a rare word *infractus,* 'unbroken.'

1329. dabant ruinas, 'wrought ruin'; l. 1340 'fera facta dedere '.

1330. transversa, 'by shying' or 'swerving to the side would try to avoid '.

exibant, with the accusative, is not uncommon in the sense of avoiding; so in Verg. *Aen*. v. 438 ' corpore tela modo atque oculis vigilantibus exit ', and in xi. 750 'vim viribus exit '.

adactūs, 'the thrusts' or 'gashes', a common meaning of *adigo,* though **adactus** is ἄπ. λεγ.

1331. iumenta : tame animals, 'equi mulique atque asini.' We have a similar description of rearing in Verg. *Aen*. x. 892 'tollit se arrectum quadrupes et calcibus auras verberat '.

58

1332. **ab nervis succisa,** 'hamstrung,' used of men or horses. **ab nervis**=*a parte nervorum*.

1333. **concidere . . . :** Verg. *Aen*. v. 447 ' ipse gravis graviterque ad terram pondere vasto concidit', of the crashing fall of the mighty boxer Entellus.

1334. **ante :** adverbial, to be taken with **putabant.** For the assonance of **domi domitos** cf. the quotation from Vergil on l. 1333. In l. 392 we have ' certamine . . . cernere certant ', ii. 539 ' penitus penetrari ', iii. 753 ' fera saecla ferarum '.

1336. Notice the emphatic asyndeton as in ll. 1192, 1372, 1448-9.

1337. **reducere:** scanned as *redducere* ; cf. *relligio* and *relliquiae* for the sake of metre.

1339. **male mactae.** Munro takes *mactae* as a past participle of an obsolete *macĕre*; cf. *permacĕre*. Ennius has ' permaceat paries'; cf. *macellum*. Others hold it to be a syncopated form of *mactatus* from *macto*. Duff distinguishes it clearly from the participle of the obsolete *magĕre*, found in the phrase ' macte virtute', well done.

1340. **fera facta :** the object of **dedere** ; cf. l. 1329.

1341-6. MSS. have six lines which Munro considers spurious. Duff says ' they are clearly a collection of tags from other parts of the poem, interpolated by some ignorant copyist'. Others retain the first three lines and reject the three following.

> si⟨c⟩ fuit ut facerent : sed vix adducor ut, ante
> quam commune malum ficret foedumque, futurum
> non quierint animo praesentire atque videre.
> et magis id possis factum contendere in omni
> in variis mundis varia ratione creatis (as in l. 528)
> quam certo atque uno terrarum quolibet orbi.

The general meaning is ' such was their conduct : yet I can scarcely believe that they would not be able to foresee and forecast the probable disaster even before it actually happened. And one would find it easier to imagine it happening under general circumstances anywhere in the universe rather than in any particular world,' the idea being that if a phenomenon is uncommon somewhere it must be common somewhere else in order to preserve the equilibrium (ἰσονομία).

1347. **voluerunt :** the subject is the whole of l. 1349.

1348. **ipsique perire,** ' though they themselves should perish' : they did not wish to die. Duff quotes Thuc. iii. 40 οἱ μὴ ξὺν προφάσει τινὰ κακῶς ποιοῦντες ἐπεξέρχονται καὶ διόλλυνται, i. e. attack their foes at the cost of their own lives.

1350. **nexilis:** i.e. of skins tied together, and still earlier of plaited reeds or long leaves.

1351. **tela,** ' the web,' the threads of which were fastened vertically to the yarnbeam (*scapi*) below and above to the *iugum* and separated alternately by the heddles (*insilia*), of which there were two, so as to leave a diamond-shaped space through which the shuttles (*radii*) passed horizontally : the spindles (*fusi*) held the thread. See cut on p. 60.

    lēvia, ' polished.'

1352. gigni, 'be made.'

1353. insilia, ἅπ. λεγ.

sonantes: the yarnbeams resounded as they swung between the uprights.

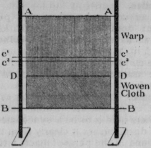

A A the *iugum* to which the vertical threads (the warp) were made fast; *B B* the *scapus* or yarnbeam on which the cloth is built; *D D* the line where the warp meets the cloth already ,woven; *c¹c¹c²c²* are the *insilia* which pass through the vertical threads alternately and so form a diamond-shaped passage through which the shuttle and weft travel horizontally.

1354. In Egypt in Herodotus' time men did the weaving, while the women did business and traded, Herod. ii. 35 αἱ μὲν γυναῖκες ἀγοράζουσι καὶ καπηλεύουσι, οἱ δὲ ἄνδρες κατ' οἴκους ἐόντες ὑφαίνουσι.

1357. vitio vertere. Cf. l. 1294 'versa in opprobrium'.

vitio: predicative dative; cf. l. 1235.

1359. pariter: i.e. *cum agricolis.* Cf. l. 1272 'pariter durum sufferre laborem'.

1361. specimen, 'model'; so in l. 186 'si non ipsa dedit specimen natura creandi'.

insitionis, ' grafting.'

rerum depends on *creatrix.*

1363. arboribus: ablative of place whence.

caducae=*cadentes.*

bacae: especially olives and arbute-berries.

1364. tempestiva, 'in due season.'

examina, ' swarms ' or ' patches of young shoots '.

pullorum, or *pullulus,* rare in this sense for *surculus.*

subter: adverb; see note on l. 1324.

1365. unde: either (1) 'and stimulated by this success'; or (2)= *a natura discentes,* 'imitating nature again,' when for instance they noticed mistletoe grafting itself on apple-trees.

libitumst, 'they conceived the wish to.'

1366. Cf. l. 935.

defodere=*inserere.*

1367. aliam atque aliam, ' another and yet another tillage of the plot so dear to them.'

agelli: an affectionate diminutive.

1368. mansuescere: here transitive governing *fructus.* They

saw that careful working of the soil improved the fruits by gradually
removing the roughness natural to them in their wild condition.
terram is an alteration for *terrā*.

1370. **in dies**: see note on l. 1279.

succedere, ' retreat higher up the hillside.'

1371. **infra**: an adverb; see note on *subter*, l. 1324.

1372. Notice the asyndeton and cf. ll. 1192, 1336, 1448-9.

lacus, ' water tanks', or perhaps ' dew ponds'.

rivos, ' irrigation channels.'

laeta, 'luxuriant,' as in l. 921.

1374. ' And to admit a grey-green ribbon of olive-trees to run
between and mark the plots, spreading over . . .'

caerula: the stock epithet of olives, referring to the leaves of
the trees. The Greeks use epithets of the same signification,
Pind. *Ol.* iii. 23 γλαυκόχροα κόσμον ἐλαίας : Soph. *O. C.* 701 γλαυκᾶς
φύλλον ἐλαίας.

inter ... currere: tmesis ; cf. note on l. 883.

plăga: a band or zone.

1377. **quae**: governed by *ornant*.

intersita: with fruit-trees planted between.

pomis: of different kinds of trees, apples, pears, cherries, figs,
grapes, berries, nuts, &c.

1378. **arbustis,** ' plantations.' Munro : ' Lucretius uses *arbusta*
continually for *arbores*, never *arbustis* for *arboribus* which suits his
verse : *arbustis* therefore has here its usual meaning.'

circum: adverb ; see note on *subter*, l. 1324.

1379. **imitarier**: see note on *molirier*, l. 934. It is subject to *fuit*.

1380. **ante fuit,** ' it was the custom to . . .' ; cf. note on l. 1297.

1381. **concelebrare,** ' to frequent,' as in i. 4 ' terras concelebras ',
so ' to practise frequently ', here ' to sing.'

1382. **zephyri** depends on **sibila,** ' the whistling ' (=ψιθύρισμα),
an irregular plural found in poets, *sibili* occurring in Cicero ; cf. *ioci*,
ioca, and others.

cava calamorum. Cf. l. 772 ' caerula mundi ' ; Verg. *Aen.*
v. 180 ' summa scopuli '.

1383. **cicutas**: properly hemlock stalks, used for pipes also in
Verg. *Ecl.* ii. 36 ' est mihi disparibus septem compacta cicutis fistula '.

agrestis: accusative masculine.

1385. **pulsata**: of the fingers pressing on the flute holes.

1386. **repertas,** ' which greet us,' agreeing with *querelas*.

1387. **otia dia,** ' abodes of unearthly calm,' preternatural stillness.

dius has two meanings, ' bright,' divine.' Two lines follow here
which are identical with ll. 1454-5 and have been wrongly inserted.

1390. **ollis**: see note on l. 1291.

1391. **cum satiate cibi**=*iam satiatis cibo*. Munro quotes the
line so frequent in Homer : ἐπεὶ πόσιος καὶ ἐδητύος ἐξ ἔρον ἕντο.

tum=*post epulas*.

cordi. Roby, *Lat. Gram.* Pt. ii. xl, predicative dative. Duff
takes it as a locative ' at heart '.

1392-6. These lines resemble very closely ii. 29-33.

> cum tamen inter se prostrati in gramine molli
> propter aquae rivum sub ramis arboris altae
> non magnis opibus iucunde corpora curant,
> praesertim cum tempestas arridet et anni
> tempora conspergunt viridantis floribus herbas.

1394. iucunde habebant=*iucundi reficiebant* or *curabant* as in l. 939.

1395. tempestas, 'weather.'

tempora, 'seasons.'

1398. consuerant: contracted for *consueverant.*

1399. plexis coronis floribus, 'with wreaths plaited with flowers.' Cf. Catull. lxiv. 284 'hos (flores) plexos tulit ille corollis'.

lascivia, 'pure lightness of heart.' In this sense *monebat* would usually be followed by *ut* with subj.

1401. extra numerum, 'out of step and time.' In l. 1409 we have 'numerum servare'.

1402. duriter et duro: cf. l. 950 'umida saxa, umida saxa', and note ; Verg. *Aen.* v. 447 'ipse gravis graviterque concidit'.

1404. vigebant, 'were in high honour.'

1405. hinc : *a musa agresti.*

solacia somni, 'a consolation for want of sleep ;' so in Aesch. *Ag.* 17 ὕπνου ἀντίμολπον ἄκος.

1406. ducere, flectere, percurrere: infinitives used as substantives.

1407. percurrere lābro. Cf. iv. 588 'unco saepe lăbro calamos percurrit hiantis'.

1408. unde haec accepta, 'these traditions received from them,' i. e. from the countrymen above.

vigiles: either (1) sentinels in camp, or (2) the fire brigade in Rome, of which there is a vivid account in Petron. 78 and Juv. *Sat.* xiv. 305-6.

1409. numerum servare, 'to keep the proper time' ; cf. l. 1401. Munro reads *recens* for MS. reading *genus.*

hilo: *hilum* is the primitive form of *nihilum.* We find in Festus 'hilum putant esse quod grano fabae adhaeret, ex quo nihil et nihilum'. Ablative of difference as *multo* in l. 1445.

1411. silvestre, 'rough,' 'uncouth.'

1412. praesto: pleonastic with *adest* ; but cf. l. 604 'est etiam quoque', l. 1169 'quippe etenim'.

pollere, 'to be best.'

1414. There are three ways of taking this line : (1) as Wakefield 'illaque melior res posterior reperta perdit sensus' ; (2) 'posteriorque res melior perdit illa reperta et immutat sensus' ; (3) as Munro 'posteriorque res melior reperta perdit illa (i. e. priora)', 'as a rule the later discovery of something better spoils the taste for former things.' The last way seems to be the clearest and best.

1415. sensus ad . . ., 'our feelings towards all that is old-fashioned.'

1416. glandis: objective genitive after *odium.* Cf. Numbers xxi. 5 'our soul loatheth this light bread.'

illa = *priora*.

1417. strata: with **herbis**. Cf. ll. 971-2.

aucta, 'heaped up.'

1418. Cf. ll. 954, 1011, of the times when such clothing was still unknown and when it was invented.

pellis: the genitive depends on **vestis**.

1419. quam reor, 'though I can well imagine that clothing of skins in the early days of its discovery provoked such envy . . .'

1420. letum: accusat. after *obiret*: **insidiis**, ablative of manner.

qui gessit, sc. *pellem ferinam*.

1421. et tamen, 'and yet after all.'

sanguine: with *disperiisse*, 'was spoiled.'

convertere, intransitive; see note on l. 831.

1425. quo, 'and in this matter.'

resedit: from *resideo*.

1426. Cf. ll. 953-7.

1427. carere: substantival infinitive, subject to *laedit*.

1428. auro signisque apta: (1) hendiadys, 'decked with figures embroidered in gold;' (2) 'decked with gold spangles and embroidered figures.' For the hendiadys cf. Verg. *Aen*. xi. 72 'geminas vestes auroque ostroque rigentes'. *Aen*. i. 648 'pallam signis auroque rigentem'. So too in English, Byron's *Sennacherib*, 'his cohorts were gleaming with purple and gold.'

1429. dum, 'if only.'

plebeia: sc. *vestis*.

sit; sc. *nobis*.

For the sentiment cf. Hor. *Sat*. i. 3. 13 'sit mihi . . . toga quae defendere frigus quamvis crassa queat'.

1430. incassum frustraque. Cf. 1002 'temere incassum frustra'.

1432. quae finis: see note on l. 826 : (1) 'object'; (2) 'limit.'

1433. quoad: monosyllabic; cf. note on l. 1033; 'up to what point genuine pleasure continues to increase',

1434. id: i. e. this misconception of pleasure has launched the vessel of man's life into a sea of trouble.

in altum: there is a similar metaphor in Aesch. *P. V.* 746 δυσχείμερόν γε πέλαγος ἀτηρᾶς δύης, and again in 563 χειμαζόμενον, 'with troubles tempest-tost.' So in Shakespeare 'a sea of troubles'.

1435. Cf. l. 1289 'belli miscebant fluctus'.

1436. vigiles: to be taken with **sol et luna**.

magnum versatile: for the asyndeton see note on l. 1064.

templum: as in l. 1188, where see note; 'the vault' or 'space of heaven'. So also in ll. 1204-5.

1437. circum: adverb; see note on *subter*, l. 1324. Notice the liquid *l* alliteration of the line.

1438. perdocuere. Aeschylus gives us a similar description of the gradual acquisition of the knowledge of the stars and seasons in *P. V.* 454 ἦν δ' οὐδὲν αὐτοῖς οὔτε χείματος τέκμαρ οὔτ' ἀνθεμώδους ἦρος οὔτε καρπίμου θέρους βέβαιον, ἀλλ' ἄτερ γνώμης τὸ πᾶν ἔπρασσον, ἔστε δή σφιν ἀντολὰς ἐγὼ ἄστρων ἔδειξα τάς τε δυσκρίτους δύσεις.

1439. rem, 'system' = *rerum naturam*.

1439. ordine certo : the knowledge that everything occurred in its proper order gave men a starting-point on which they might base their calculations about the seasons.

1441. divisa discretaque : pleonastic, ' portioned off and marked out by boundaries.'

1442. florebat. The Greeks used the same metaphor, Aesch. *Ag.* 659 ὁρῶμεν ἀνθοῦν πέλαγος Αἰγαῖον νεκροῖς ἀνδρῶν Ἀχαιῶν ναυτικοῖς τ' ἐρειπίοις : Eur. *Iph. Taur.* 300 ὥσθ' αἱματηρὸν πέλαγος ἐξανθεῖν ἁλός, ' was studded with.' In this passage the verb no doubt also contains an idea of the prosperity of the sea trade.

puppibus ; urbes is Munro's correction for *propter odores* in the MSS., a reading which makes no sense.

1443. Men began to realize that peace with their neighbours was preferable to war.

1444. res gestas, ' the deeds of men,'= κλέα ἀνδρῶν, ' songs of the feats of heroes, with which the history of most nations begins ' (Duff).

1445-8. Cf. ll. 324-31, where the argument is as follows : If there had been no beginning to the world, why does history begin only with the wars of Thebes and Troy ? How does it happen that the achievements of so many heroes are buried in silence ? Surely then either the world is young or its history and civilization have suffered frequent interruptions and occasional annihilation, only however to spring up again.

multo : ablative of difference as *hilo*, l. 1409.

elementa = the letters of the alphabet.

1447. vestigia : traces of ancient civilization, i. e. from prehistoric buildings or from figures drawn and scratched on rocks before writing was invented or partly from oral tradition that seems well founded and logical.

1448-9. Notice the asyndeton and cf. ll. 1336, 1372. In these two lines we have a list of the useful arts.

1450-1. Here follow the finer arts which are the true luxuries of life, **praemia.**

funditus, ' without exception.'

daedala, ' well-wrought,' used in a passive sense as in Verg. *Georg.* iv. 179 ' daedala fingere tecta '.

polire : substantival infinitive.

1452. usus, ' practice.'

1453. pedetemptim progredientis : as in l. 533 ' pedetemptim progredientis '.

1454. unumquicquid=*unumquidque*, ' each separate thing ' : so in Plaut. *Trin.* iv. 2. 39 ' unumquicquid percontabere '. For ll. 1454-5 see note on l. 1387.

protrahit in medium. Cf. l. 1158 ' protraxe in medium '.

1456. alid : for *aliud*, as in l. 1305 ' one after another,' i. e. one developed from another.

cordi' depends on *artibus*, ' by the inventions of their mind ' : *cor* is used of the intellect, which the Romans imagined was seated in the heart.

INDEX

ablative in -i: labi, 930; igni, 953, 1250, 1254; of description, 838, 879, 968, 1274, 1277.

accusative, of exclamation, 1194; of reference, 844, 1053.

adhaesu, 842.

adit = implorat, 1229.

alid = aliud, 1305, 1456.

alio et, 1066; cf. 1260.

alituum, 801.

alliteration, *see under* b, c, l, m, p, s, u, v, and Introd. p. 5.

alsia, 1015.

alter = alius, 835.

ambiguity, 1414.

amicitiem (for -iam), 1019.

androgynum, 839.

anguimanus, 1303.

animal, 823.

animantum, 855.

a parvis, 977.

ἅπαξ λεγόμενα : adactus, 1330; adhaesu, 842; auxiliatum, 1040; barbigeras, 900; baubantur, 1071; deplexae, 1321; insilia, 1353; levisomna, 864; lidebant, 1001 ; pennipotentum, 789 ; summatum, 1142.

apti, 808.

arbusta = arbores, 912 ; cf. 1378.

arbute trees, 941.

Argos, 864.

arsis, 1049.

assonance, 1334, 1360, 1402.

asyndeton, 1002, 1192, 1336, 1372, 1436, 1448-9.

aurea, 911.

b in alliteration, 1300.

balbe, 1022.

barbigeras, 900.

baubantur, 1071.

bis binos, 1300.

boves lucas, 1302.

bucera, 866.

c in alliteration, 1334.

Chimaera, 905.

clam id fore, 1157.

claru', with citat, 947.

complexa, passive, 922.

concelebrare, 1381.

concord, rule of, 1285.

consimilem, with genitive, 813.

convertere, intrans., 1421.

cordi esse, 1391.

cristae, of lions, 1315.

dative, ethic, 805, 1209; of possessor, 1319.

demonstrat. pronoun for relat., 898.

denique, 858.

deplexae, 1321.

dia, 1387.

discovery of fire, 953, 1015.

dogs, 864; cries of, 1063, 1070, 1071.

donec, with plpf. 997.

durare, trans., 1360.

elementa, 1445.

elephants, 1302-3.

Empedocles, 908.

epanalepsis, 949, 1190, 1402.

Epicurus, 1047, Introd. pp. 6-7.

ergo, preposition, 1246.

ethic dative, 805, 1209.

etiam atque etiam, 821.

et tamen, 1096, 1177.

evolution, 836.

exibant, trans., 1330.

faecem, metaphor, 1141.

falcis, 1294.

fear of eternal night, 972.

finem, femin., 826, 1213, 1432.

fire, discovery of, 953, 1015.

florebat puppibus, 1442.

fluctus belli, metaphor, 1289.

folliculos, 803.

foras = foris, 906.

OXFORD
PRINTED AT THE CLARENDON PRESS
BY HORACE HART, M.A.
PRINTER TO THE UNIVERSITY